Every Step You Take

A Teenager's Journey

By

Joseph M. Alicea

This book is a work of non-fiction. The events and situations are true.

ISBN: 1-4107-9910-7 (e-book)
ISBN: 1-4107-9909-3 (Paperback)
ISBN: 1-4107-9908-5 (Dust Jacket)

This book is printed on acid-free paper.

1stBooks – rev. 12/10/03

Acknowledgements

Over the many months it took to prepare this book for publication, my thoughts were open to many days gone by. I sat alone in my office at home and cried often as I wrote down the memories that fill this book. Tears also covered my eyes as I wrote while seated on airplanes during business trips. However, in spite of the tears, many smiles came too. Smiles brought on by great memories of wonderful times.

I must thank at least a few of the people whom have filled me with the strength to reach back into the years gone by and try to use what I experienced and turn it into a gift.

My wife Felicita and my three daughters, Elloise, Jeanne, and Jessica are a constant source of encouragement. My Uncle Salvador is one of my greatest mentors. Joann Cleer remains a great sounding board for my creative thought processes. Regardless of the path, my life has taken; I will always be the son of Doña Carmen Lydia Rivera. I know she loves me in her own way.

My brother Michael, my partner through childhood, I thank him for being Salt of the Salt and Pepper Twins.

The many friends I named in this book are with me always. I learned from each of them. We laughed, loved, grew up together, and took care of each other. I am proud of them and I love them dearly. Their love has always been a source of energy for me.

My gratitude also goes to the many people who have long passed from this life. My grandmother, Doña Hortensia De la Rosa, whose hands lifted me when I fell, was my greatest teacher. My Uncle Rogelio, a gentle man who called me his "Dirty Nigger." His shocking words were really words of love that came with a strong embrace and a message only he and I understood.

I sincerely hope I have made all of these special people proud of me.

Dedication

For our grandmothers' children

Contents

Foreword

My 1993 version of the Merriam-Webster's Collegiate Dictionary (Tenth Edition), gives eight definitions for the word Foreword: 1a states, "near, being at, or belonging to the forepart"; 5a - "advocating an advanced policy in the direction of what is considered progress;" 5b - "extreme, radical"; 6 - "of relating to, or getting ready for the future." This part of a book is called a Foreword and is at the beginning of the book, so that fits with the 1a definition. The other three definitions above, to my way of thinking, are a good description of the rest of the book you are holding.

Joe Alicea loves people, especially young people. He sees their potential, their fears, their challenges, their hurts, and their love. He also knows about all of these because he has lived them from his beginning on the tough streets of Bronx, New York all the way to the windowless vaults of the North American Aerospace Defense (NORAD) Complex deep inside Cheyenne Mountain, Colorado. Joe is "advocating an advanced policy" of straight talk to pre-teens and teens to help them in "getting ready for the future." To some, his stories may be "extreme, radical," but kids hate being talked down to and they want to hear and read what is real.

Joe's stories are real. They are about people he has known, and in some cases, loved. Many of these stories are painful to read, but then life can be painful. These stories are real examples of the message he is trying to get across to you, the young readers.

My suggestion is for you to read Joe's stories with an open mind and an open heart. Hear what he is telling you and use it as part of the knowledge base you draw from when you are faced with similar challenges or choices in your own lives. You have a choice. You can learn things in your life the hard, painful way or you can learn from someone else's pains and experiences and choose to do it differently.

Joe Alicea is offering you his experiences with some of the most important decisions you will face. Use those experiences as you see fit but know that he offers them to you with love as a means of helping you to get ready for your future.

Dr. C. Darlene VanEvery

Falls Church, Virginia

June 2001

Open Letters to Parents and Young Readers

Dear Parents,

I wrote this book with the sincere intent of helping young people work their way through the maze that confronts them as they transition from childhood to adulthood. The book's format places me in direct communication with young readers. However, I also wrote this book hoping to help parents have straightforward discussions with their children about some very important issues.

I wish I could say that my parents were my mentors; that they helped me prepare for adulthood. The stories you will read in this book will show that my mother and father were everything but my mentors through my youth.

This book contains many revealing stories. I have made the details of my early years along with details of the lives of many other people available to you in hopes that you use these stories as support tools for mentoring your children. Some of the topics I introduce include Culture, Teenage Sex, Violence, Friendships, Heroes, Respect, Education, and the Value of Seeking Goodness. Each of these topics is presented as candidly as possible with honest recounts of real-life experiences, the mistakes made, the lessons learned, the opportunities earned and lost, and my reflection on those experiences.

As parents, I hope that we share the view that I repeatedly enforce throughout this book; that each individual is responsible for his or her own actions. The paths we take in life are our own and the manner, in which we conduct ourselves, as we travel down those paths, is a personal choice. I hope that we seek to instill in young people the acknowledgment that the steps they take as they walk down their chosen paths define their character, their future, and their legacy.

I truly hope that you use my stories to help bridge the communication gap between the generation you represent and your children's generation. More importantly, I hope that as you discuss the subjects I present, you will take the opportunity to reach back into your youthful years and share your experiences with the young people of today. While my stories may serve you well in a support role, it is your stories that will surely connect best with your children. I wish you well in this most important human endeavor – raising children. Mentor them, guide them, help them, and love them.

Joe Alicea

Dear Young Readers,

The stories in this book are about a kid who grew up in New York City. The kid's name is Joe Alicea. This is my story!

"O.K., so you grew up in NYC. What's that mean to me?" you might ask.

Please allow me to begin answering that question with the following: I recognize that you might not come from as large a city as New York. I also recognize that the experiences I had might not even relate to anything you have experienced to date or possibly ever will. However, we do share an undeniable bond – we, as kids, past and present, have often been confused by all the stuff that confronts us during those fragile years of our youth.

Throughout this book, I will recount many of those defining moments when I was an adolescent, especially my high school years and what those years meant to me. I will share with you the good, the bad, and the ugly as straightforwardly as I can. However, as I tell you those true-life stories, don't expect me to clutter the pages of the book using the language of the streets as I used them or heard them. I feel those words would take your attention away from the joyful and sometimes harsh realities of what I experienced growing up. It is the realities, not the language, which I need to try to convey to you.

Trust me when I tell you that I'm about to share with you some of the most personal details of my years growing up in New York, details known to very few people. I am going to walk you through some of the challenges I faced and then I will introduce you to some of the survival tools I used. I will also share with you some insight to the keys that opened the doors through which I eventually experienced a life that I had never imagined.

I decided to write a book with the specific intention of addressing young boys and girls, ages twelve through seventeen. Why would I want to resurface all of these memories? My reason was very simple. Many people call those early years of life, your formative years. I will not argue with that label. Those years twisted me like a pretzel, pulled me in all directions and eventually formed the "me" I was to become. Those years were filled with some of the happiest, saddest, most confusing, emotionally awakening, scariest, challenging, and weirdest events of my life. Those years were tough, a series of endless days that were all too short.

I will admit that while my environment may have influenced me somewhat, I am not necessarily a product of that environment. Stay with me as I walk you through my years of discovery, feeling my way through the maze, and transitioning from a smart-ass street kid to a smarter, less of an ass, adult.

Everything I am about to share with you is true. I will share happy, sad, and very proud moments as well as some very shameful moments during my youth. You may not understand some of the things you are about to read. If that should happen, please do not hesitate to ask your parents, family elders or your teachers to clarify any of those foggy points for you. I also ask that as you read this book you remember I was just like you – a kid trying to grow up. I do not have any excuses. I survived.

Joe Alicea

"The soul is dyed the color of its thoughts. Think only those things that are in line with your principles and can bear the full light of day. The content of your character is your choice. Day by day, what you think, and what you do is who you become. Your integrity is your destiny…it is the light that guides your way."

Heraclites – Greek Poet and Philosopher

Chapter One
A Teenage Hero

In 1986, President Reagan ordered a military response against Libya for its part in terrorist activities that claimed the lives of several Americans. The strike, involving forces from the US Air Force, Navy, and Marine Corps, was swift; delivering a clear message to those who would chose U.S. citizens as targets.

An Air Force Captain I know very well was assigned to a remote detachment in Europe at the time of that strike. The detachment was housed in a small compound behind three fences within the confines of a small, nondescript air station well off the beaten path. The only features that made the detachment stand out from the other buildings on the air station were the three fences and the two, very large satellite dishes within the compound. If you were inquisitive enough to venture near the compound, you would immediately notice the armed security patrol, K-9 handlers, and armored personnel carriers in and around the compound. The finer details of the concertina barbed wire on those three fences and the corrugated steel and sandbag gun emplacements at each corner inside the compound, would soon catch your attention too.

Only the very daring would venture close enough to read the warning signs posted every fifty feet along the entire perimeter of the fence line. The signs read, "Deadly Force Authorized," in English and in the language of the host country. The windowless building at the base of the satellite dishes gave no hint of the detachment's mission. However, you didn't need a rocket-scientist to figure out that whatever the mission was it had to be important.

The Captain was one of five Combat Operations Crew Commanders assigned to the detachment. The crews, comprised of a Crew Commander, a Deputy Commander, electronics technicians, and a small security force worked a 24/7 crew schedule, twenty-four hours a day, seven days a week. Each crewmember knew their role in the mission. The success of his or her mission was dependent on total commitment from each crewmember. There were no exceptions to that reality.

Life was good inside that fence line. The crews would often bar-b-cue steaks or burgers for dinner or cook made-to-order omelets for breakfast before going home after a long night. Those fun things, that broke up a shift's often-boring routine, were team things; even the officers cooked and took turns washing the dishes. They celebrated Christmas and birthdays together and exchanged gifts. The teams took trips throughout Europe with their families. Whenever someone from the "States" came to visit, they always shared a night on the town and introduced the team to the visitors. When illness or tragedy struck any of the families, even the distant, stateside relatives, they comforted each other as if they were one family. They took care of each other.

The Captain was scheduled for duty the night following the attack on Libya. It was cold and raining that evening as he approached the main gate at the air station. Under normal conditions, the security personnel would salute and wave him through the gate; using personal recognition as their guide for granting access. However, nothing was normal that night. A very distinct wave of the security guard's arm brought him to a stop just short of the gate. The guard was in full battle dress; camouflaged Battle Dress Uniform (BDU), web belt with canteen, gas mask, a sidearm and ammo plus an M-16 rifle. He asked the Captain to exit the car and present identification. The Captain knew the Airman at the gate and he knew the Airman was doing his job and rank or no rank, the Captain had better produce acceptable identification if he wanted to get past the gate.

Having presented his identification, the guard rendered a very sharp salute; the Captain returned the same. The Captain was then asked to step aside while they searched his vehicle. Ignoring the rain and the chilled air, the Captain turned the vehicle's ignition off, opened the door slowly and deliberately, got out, and walked a few steps away from the vehicle. He knew what would come next.

Two other Airmen appeared; one with a dog, the other had a long pole with a large mirror attached to one end. They opened all the doors, the trunk, and the hood. They looked everywhere, including underneath the vehicle; they were very thorough.

A Staff Sergeant on the security team approached the Captain, exchanged salutes with him, and then very discretely informed him that the facility was under a higher THREATCON (Threat Condition). It may seem as though he was stating the obvious, but the Sergeant knew the Captain was the on-coming Crew Commander and the Sergeant's duty was to make sure the Crew Commander was aware of the THREATCON. This was no drill.

The search was completed and the Captain reentered his car. The Sergeant rendered another sharp salute and wished him a good evening. The Captain returned an equally sharp salute as he drove through the gate. It was going to be an interesting night.

The Captain drove onto the air station and proceeded to the remote area where the detachment was located. He parked his car in a designated area just outside the compound and well away from the compound's security fences. As he neared the outer security gate, two members of the security detail approached him and asked for identification. Both of them knew the Captain, knew of his duties on crew, yet they stopped him until he produced a second set of identification specifically required for access into the compound. Only then were salutes exchanged and the Captain allowed access through the two electronically activated gates leading to the inner building; one gate at a time, the previous gate securely closed before the next gate would open. The gates were 25 feet apart. This security detail, just like the detail at the main gate, had a tough job to do. They also knew that if they failed to follow the procedures, under these threat conditions, the Captain would direct that they be relieved of duty. No need, they did it "By the Numbers."

Combat crews go through a certain set of formalities when they perform a crew changeover. All aspects of the mission are reviewed. The past 24-hours and future activities are discussed with the old crew including mission readiness, operations, communication systems status, identification of all personnel on site, and any changes in THREATCON or DEFCON (Defense Readiness Condition). The crews posted the location of the Detachment Commander and all other key personnel on their checklists. Finally, the crews discussed how high the "PUCKER" factor was – the measure of how terrified you really are or should be.

Having completed the required changeover briefings, the Crew Commander and his Deputy Crew Commander took charge of the detachment and settled in for the night. The Deputy was a young First Lieutenant from New Jersey named Wayne Jasinski. Lieutenant Jasinski verified the Mission System's readiness while the Captain read the reams of message traffic from their headquarters. The results of the bombing attack on Libya were covered in detail. The US Armed Forces Radio and Television Service broadcasts had given them the news and pictures earlier in the day. The Crew Commander's immediate concern was the threat of a hostile response from Libya or Libyan sympathizers. It would be hard for the crew to get a warm and comfortable feeling over that threat while sitting in a cinderblock building, surrounded by tall, barbed wire fences, heavy wooded areas on two sides and known sympathizers in country.

Around midnight, the crew had a planned maintenance activity that allowed the crew commanders to leave their control center and stretch their legs in the administration area of the building. The detachment had a small kitchenette there where the crews kept the coffee and munchies. Unlike the rest of the crew, the Captain and the Lieutenant were dressed in their normal uniform of the day; dark blue pants and a light blue oxford shirt with their rank on the shirts' epaulets. Their BDUs were stored in mobility bags inside the facility; however, they chose not to wear them. As the Captain entered the kitchenette, he decided to make some hot chocolate for the guards standing watch outside.

As the Captain stood at the counter of the kitchenette, heating a pot of water on a hot plate, Lieutenant Jasinski walked up to him and asked what he was doing. "I'm making hot chocolate for the guards in the gun emplacements," said the Captain.

"With all due respect Sir, are you nuts?" With a bit of anxiety in his voice, Lieutenant Jasinski then reminded the Captain that, "We're not exactly surrounded by friendly people out there." Lieutenant Jasinski watched the Captain as he prepared four cups, put them on a tray, and proceeded to walk outside without wearing anything to cover his light blue shirt and rank.

The rain had let up but it was still very cool and damp. The Captain walked to the furthest two emplacements first. Salutes were not exchanged. The guards kept their eyes on the perimeter fence line, not on him. He spoke with each of the guards for a bit and then moved on. No doubt, there was not any shortage of tension. There is a fine line between fear and tension and the Captain prayed that tonight these young Airmen would not face the ultimate test. The Captain then walked over to the third emplacement and did the same thing, trying to put everyone at ease.

Senior Airman Kim Bugley occupied the fourth emplacement. She was the same age as the Captain's oldest daughter who was in the Navy and stationed in Spain during that period. The sight of Airman Bugley made him think of his daughter's safety and potential call for the ultimate sacrifice. Airman Bugley was all of five feet, one inch tall, weighing about 105 pounds. Yet, there she stood, in full battle dress, wearing a flak vest with two ammo belts crossing her chest, a nine millimeter semiautomatic sidearm, a gas mask hooked to her web belt, a grenade launcher attached to her M-16, and a box of grenades at her feet. Her total weight had to be near two hundred pounds; she was loaded for bear!

Airman Bugley gave the Captain a quick glance and a smile when he approached. He could see that she was as nervous as everyone else was in the compound. The Captain was not sure if it was the cold, wet night or the tension that had her lower lip quivering but either one was understandable. "Sir, do you think it's safe for you to be out here dressed like that?" Airman Bugley asked as she drank the hot chocolate, still concentrating on the perimeter.

7

"No," replied the Captain, "but that's what I have you here for."

They talked a bit more and as Airman Bugley finished her cup of chocolate, he asked her what she would do if terrorists came over the outer fence.

"Sir, I'd let loose the dogs," she replied.

"What if they made it to the second fence?" he returned.

"Sir, I'd lay down a blanket of fire and launch grenades," she said with clear certainty.

Then he said to her, "I guess if they make it to the third fence, I'd have to surrender."

Airman Bugley turned to her Crew Commander with a cold stare and absolutely no quivering of her lip and said, "SIR, over my dead body!"

I have told that story many times and in many different forums over the years. I have presented the story to senior corporate and government employees as an example of good leadership. I have told the story to young officers and enlisted personnel as an example of dedication and service to one's country. Today, I present the story to you from its most basic perspective – it is a story about a teenage hero, a simple account of bravery by a young woman, a nineteen year old.

I recount that story easily because the memory of that night has remained fresh in my mind over the years. I am the Captain in that story and I can still feel the cold dampness on my uniform. I still remember the look on that young woman's face as she offered her life for the safety of others. Undeniably, that night was one of the most memorable moments in my twenty-one years in the US Air Force. I will be forever grateful. Thanks Kim, Wayne, and the rest of the Communications Squadron Operations and Security teams.

That is the first of many stories I will be sharing with you throughout this book. I hope that the stories will shed a little bit of light on some important questions. How do teenagers, such as Kim Bugley, come to such a sense of service, honor, and commitment at such an early point in their life? How do the thousands of young men and women, sailors, soldiers and airman, serving their country and the world in today's war against terrorism, come to such a point of personal sacrifice at such an early age?

Maybe you know someone named Kim who is in the military. Maybe someone in your neighborhood is a Fireman, a Police Officer, a Nurse, or a Teacher. Ask them what the significant events and influences were in their lives that set the paths they have taken.

"Character cannot be developed in ease and quiet.
Only through the experience of trial and suffering can
the soul be strengthened, ambition inspired, and
success achieved."

Helen Keller

Chapter Two
And So, The Story Begins

It was a surreal moment, I opened my eyes and I immediately
recognized the ceiling above the bed I was in; it was the same hospital
ward my brother Michael had been in a few years earlier. I reached
out and touched the bed around me; the sheets were drawn tight
against me. Then I touched my body; I had tubes stuck in my arms
and a bandage around the top of my head. I was aware of all of this in
an instant. In an instant, I knew I must be hurt, hurt enough to be
laying in a bed at Fordham Hospital in the Bronx. I also knew it was
Christmas Day, 1964.

I did not hear any sounds at first; but, as my mind cleared
from the deep sleep I must have been in, I started to hear voices.
Bernie Matos' voice was the first sound that filtered into my head. I
kept hearing him telling me not to take the bandage off my head.
Well, that is exactly what I did. The bandage felt like a turban and I

just yanked it off my head and threw it across the hospital ward in the direction of Bernie's voice. So much for the bandage!

I was mad. I could not focus my eyes very well so I could not identify any faces, just voices. "Damn it Bernie, stop barking at me!"

"Joe, we were in an accident. Everybody was hurt a little bit but you're the worst one off," he said.

"Thanks for the news Bernie."

My head just would not clear up and my eyes refused to focus. Then I caught an image of a dark figure that I immediately identified and I called out, "Father!" I was right; it was a priest.

He came closer to my bed, leaned forward, and said, "You need to rest my son. You've been in an accident and you're in very bad shape. The doctors think you might not make it." He hesitated a moment and then said, "Son, you're going to die."

The priest held my hand and then asked me if I would like him to hear my confession. I then made what I thought was my last confession as he administered the Sacrament for the Dead and Dying.

Eleven hours earlier, I had been at a party; the Alvarez sisters really knew how to throw a party. Their parties always had the right ingredients: slow, make-out music, and lots of booze. I remember dancing most of the evening with my girlfriend, Sonia Alicea (no relation then and definitely none now). The hot and sexy tunes of Smoky Robinson and the Miracles, the Platters, plus Little Anthony and the Imperials mixed very well with all the rum and cola I was drinking. We danced and drank for hours and then left the party.

Seven of us headed for Bernie's neighborhood church where we planned to attend midnight mass. The last thing I remember of those previous eleven hours was getting into Bernie's car and sitting in the back seat. Sonia was with me and my arms were around her.

Eleven hours ago, it was Christmas Eve. Eleven hours ago, I was a fifteen-year old kid trying to act as an adult, thinking I was cool. Eleven hours ago, my life was in my hands, my world held lots of promise, and the future was so bright I needed shades. Eleven hours ago, I was not dying.

I still remember making that last confession. I remember the priest and I remember what happened when he handed me a mirror I had begged him for; I needed to see my face. The last thing I saw just before I lapsed back into unconsciousness was the face of a once-good looking kid. The mirror's image was still covered with dried blood; it was scarred and stitched together at the cheek, ear, and forehead.

There was a very unnatural bald spot above the left side of my forehead. That spot is where the surgeons had to cut into my skull in order to stop the hemorrhage that threatened my life. I was a mess and I was dying.

I regained consciousness twenty-four hours later. My grandmother, Doña Hortensia, my aunt, Maria Dolores, and my mother, Carmen Lydia, were at my side; my mother was praying. I did not know what to say to comfort her so I told her I was hungry. The hospital would not allow her to get me any solid food but they did allow her to give me some apple juice. Grandma just laid her hand on my chest and prayed too. Tears filled her eyes and mine.

The damage to my body was extensive. My face was so badly scarred that even Michael, my brother, had trouble recognizing me when he entered the hospital ward. My left leg was broken just above the ankle and I had bruised tendons in my foot and knee. If I survived, it would take months before I could walk. My skull was fractured from my forehead all the way to the back of my head. If I survived, it would take months before the headaches went away. My left ear was torn halfway off and you could easily see the scar; it was a dark blue seam. If I survived, it would take plastic surgery to remove the scars.

The scars were dark blue because the operating room staff did not expect me to survive the trauma. They had stitched me up without cleaning the wounds, my broken leg was left untreated, and the other cuts and bruises were stitched but not bandaged.

I lost so much blood at the scene of the accident that all the clothes I was wearing that night, including my shoes, had to be thrown out. Sixty-four stitches, a scarred face and a badly broken leg were the Christmas gifts I gave my family in 1964.

How did I manage to make such a mess of myself in one night? Easy, I just made one simple, dumb-ass move by getting into a car with a bunch of not-so-sober teenagers and driving onto a busy highway. The driver only had a learner's permit and he had been drinking. The person who was supposed to be driving was well into a few too many glasses of rum and coke. The girlfriend of the unlicensed driver amused herself by sucking his earlobe while he tried to maneuver the car through traffic. Oh yeah, she had had quite a few glasses of cheap wine too before we got into the car.

I was one of the four dummies sitting in the backseat, two boys, two girls, and lots of booze. Four kids making out and not really concerned with the fact that we were speeding down a highway in the hands of a guy who was trying to figure out how to drive straight while his girlfriend stuck her tongue into his ear. That's when we hit the wall, then struck another car just before we went off an embankment. Our car came to rest after it flipped over three times; a big Ford that ended up looking like a small Volkswagen.

Hey, we were indestructible! Yeah, right. Medical science had come a long way since Humpty Dumpty had his great fall. Today, doctors can piece you back together. Well they may have put the pieces of my body back together, but it was up to me to keep my head on straight.

Up to the moment I stepped into that car, my life was filled with endless possibilities. Up to that moment, I had foolishly failed to recognize that every decision I had faced in life had been like a series of forks in the road. Each fork was not just a two-lane, right or left choice but an endless selection of choices and each choice had an untold number of possibilities. Consequently, there I was, a fifteen-years-old kid in a hospital bed, dying because of my foolish choices.

Endless choices with endless possibilities stretching from horizon to horizon; forget that! If it is true that it is only after you have made a choice and taken a step in a given direction that your life takes a more recognizable shape, then I had obviously made the worst possible choices the night of December 24, 1964. Those decisions, those steps, set in motion beginnings, endings and everything in between for me and for many of those I loved and cared for.

The accident was a significant turning point in my life – I tripped and fell. I need to take you through the pages of my life before the accident – those things that led me to my deathbed. Then I will take you through the pages that followed the accident – those things that led to where I am today.

"You can complain because roses have thorns, or you can rejoice because thorns have roses."

Ziggy

Chapter Three
No Silver Spoons

The title of this book, Every Step You Take, implies forward motion. However, before we move forward, I need to take you back in time, to a time before I was born. The purpose of this chapter is to paint a picture for you of the cultures, customs, beliefs, and traditions that filled my world.

Consider this insight; my world, just like yours, began long before we were born. The world we were born into is a world that was already crafted by history and many external factors.

I wish my brothers and I had that insight when we were teenagers. If we had, we probably would have been more appreciative of our elder's sacrifices and achievements and more receptive of the role their customs and traditions played in their lives. Unfortunately, much of what I'm about to share with you wasn't clear to me at an early age. Sadly, I was in my twenties before the stories of my family's past took a more mature meaning and significance in my life. Allow me to present to you a bit of family history.

The town of Yabucoa, where my grandmother was born, is in the southeast region of Puerto Rico and not far from the coastal village of Arroyo. It was on the shores of Arroyo that in July 1898 American troops led by Major General Nelson A. Miles landed and raised the Stars and Stripes, the U.S. Flag. The landing would signify the end of the Spanish-American War and the four hundred years of rule from Madrid, Spain of the people of Puerto Rico.

The United States had taken possession of Puerto Rico with minimal resistance from its inhabitants. During the centuries of conquest, Puerto Ricans had only received a small measure of autonomy from Spain. The Spanish had mismanaged the natural resources of its colony and enslaved its people. The arrival of American troops marked the hopeful end to the virtual devastation, by Spain and other rival nations, of the island's precious resources. The switch to American sovereignty was received as a breath of fresh air, a new beginning.

Years later, the hopes and aspirations of many Puerto Ricans would again be bolstered by the Jones Act of 1917 that granted U.S. citizenship to all the people of Puerto Rico. These new freedoms were not granted without struggle. Men and women in the United States and Puerto Rico, including members of my grandmother's family, campaigned vigorously for many years to win the acceptance of native Puerto Ricans as U.S. citizens. Puerto Rican immigration to the United States began, in earnest, with the granting of citizenship.

My grandmother was born on January 11, 1903. She was the fifth of twelve children, all born and raised within those turbulent times of transition and national identity. She was born into a family of comfortable means and of long-standing traditions. Comfortable, as defined in Puerto Rico in 1903, meant that her parents were able to feed the children and keep a roof over their heads. Her mother was a homemaker, her father owned a small construction company.

My maternal great grandmother was Francisca Martinez de la Rosa. Her lineage was a straight path back to the Canary Islands of Spain. The Martinez family had sailed to the New World in the early 19th century. My maternal great grandfather was Felipe De la Rosa. His lineage, however, had two paths; one led to the native Taíno Indians who lived on the island long before Columbus landed. The other path led to the cargo hold of Spanish slave ships and to tribal Africa. That later path was not common knowledge to this author's generation and was not revealed to me until I was twenty-five years old.

Growing up, maturing, and raising a family during the early 1900's was no easy task for my great grandmother. Each day was a struggle; every bowl of rice and beans was a blessing. The men of the house had the responsibility of providing for the family. The idea of women working outside of the home was unacceptable by all of the island's customs and cultures. Such a mindset was created long before Hortensia was born.

Somehow, that mindset was never reflected in Hortensia's independent strength of spirit. As she grew, Hortensia developed the attitude that while it may be a man's role to provide, it certainly was the woman's role to make sure that the family was indeed provided

19

for. Her parents, especially her brothers and three former husbands could easily attest to the strength of Hortensia's resolve when it came to taking care of her family.

The choices one had for travel from Puerto Rico to the U.S. mainland, in the 1940's, were limited. World War II had depleted many of the resources necessary for national and international travel. Domestic airlines were still in their infancy and only a few commercial carriers provided scheduled flights from Puerto Rico. Consequently, only the affluent flew from Puerto Rico to the mainland. However, if one was willing, you could wait on a standby list and travel at a discounted fare. Traveling by boat was often the only option for poor families.

However limited the travel options were, the end of WW II marked the beginning of a mass exodus of Puerto Ricans to various parts of the United States. The one destination chosen by most of this new era of immigrants was New York City. New York had the same magnetism for Puerto Ricans as it had for countless millions of Europeans who immigrated to America since the turn of the twentieth century. Jobs and housing were available. Schools and hospitals were open to everyone. Opportunity was knocking on every door. And yes, "The streets were paved with gold!" [An often-heard expression by hopeful immigrants from all countries referring to the vast opportunities available in the United States]

Doña Hortensia was forty years old when she made her exodus to the New World. She had already been married and widowed as well as scarred by two other tragic relationships. Her strength helped her survive the depression; dark days that almost consumed the United States in the 1930's, and nearly devastated Puerto Rico as well. Doña Hortensia and her children had survived those years alone. The De la Rosa family had gone through an upheaval, especially amongst the greediest of her siblings who were trying to gain control of the then, well-established De la Rosa businesses.

Doña Hortensia had long ago established her independence and refused to humble herself or her children. She envisioned a better life and no sacrifice would be too big for her to handle. A few long and difficult years of working as a domestic, cooking, cleaning, sewing, and she had saved enough money to book passage, via the waiting list, for herself and her son, Salvador, to America. Her two daughters would remain in Puerto Rico, under the care of their older brother, until she could afford to have them join her in New York. Doña Hortensia and Salvador left aboard a Pan American Clipper to Miami. They then boarded a northbound train on a long, grueling ride to New York.

Doña Hortensia and her brother Francisco, "Paco," were inseparable. She had been more like a mother to him than a sister. Their mother had done her best to keep up with all of the children's needs. However, Hortensia, even as a child herself, was the one that took care of Paco. She fed, bathed, clothed, and nurtured him until he was capable of taking care of himself. Their bond was closer than the bond among any of the other children. They even had pet names for

21

each other, some of which were vulgar. Those names would infuriate the elders in the family, something that seemed to please them both.

Paco was her most ardent supporter, especially in matters concerning her right to live her life as she chose, independent and free to pick her own course. He was also the first to leave for the New World and as soon as he left Puerto Rico, the rift between Doña Hortensia and the rest of the family widened into a chasm.

Paco settled in New York City's upper West Side. He had arrived in New York at a time when the city's skyline was starting to fill up with monstrous skyscrapers. Paco was a skilled construction worker. His childhood had been spent on the construction sites where his father and older brothers worked. He also had the advantage of having a very dark complexion and wavy, jet-black hair, a carry over from the family's Taíno heritage. His skills and color helped him ease into a choice segment of construction work in New York City as a high-rise steelworker. American Indians had long been the majority among the few who dared to risk their lives on the steel girders high above the city streets.

Paco was the one who met Doña Hortensia at Penn Station on 34th Street in Manhattan. He recognized that his sister's new life would be full of struggles, struggles that would certainly overwhelm most people. He was there to see that they didn't. The bond that would grow between brother and sister would never be broken, neither in life nor in death.

Doña Hortensia and Salvador lived with Paco for a short time until she found a small apartment. By then she had found two jobs and was planning the arrival of the rest of the family. The apartment wasn't much, a cold-water flat on the West Side of Manhattan. The place was cold but affordable and safe for her and Salvador. She enrolled him in school as quickly as possible; there was no time to waste in this new life.

The available jobs were diverse and physically demanding, however the war had opened many doors for women; door to jobs usually held by men. Doña Hortensia worked at the Taft Hotel as a maid during the day and at the Brooklyn Navy Yard at night as a machinists' helper. She vowed to maintain this rugged pace until her entire family was in New York. The war would not end for another two years.

Following the war, fleets of WWII Liberty-class cargo ships were pressed into commercial service. One of those ships, the "Marine Tiger," provided regular passage from Puerto Rico to New York City. The Marine Tiger was part of a fleet of vessels that brought fruit, vegetables, coffee, tobacco, and spices from the Caribbean to the United States. Sailing to America on the Marine Tiger, often called the "Banana Boat," would soon become the recognizable expression and underlying insult for identifying immigrants from the Caribbean. Calling someone a Marine Tiger quickly became the ultimate insult used by Puerto Ricans to identify someone who had sailed to America and betrayed their heritage.

Doña Hortensia's two daughters, Dolores and Carmen; along with Carmen's husband, Alberto Cabrera and their son, Raphael would be the first of the family to come to America aboard the Marine

Tiger. Doña Hortensia paid for the passage. Her eldest son, Rogelio, was to have been aboard as well; however, he had taken the money and gambled it away. Months later, Doña Hortensia again sent him the money for the voyage. The money was accompanied with a threat that she would forever abandon him if he failed to arrive in New York within three weeks. Two weeks later, Doña Hortensia had her family with her.

Her dreams had begun to materialize.

I was born on a hot and humid day in August 1949. My mother went into labor early and I was born in her eighth month of pregnancy. I must have been in a hurry as my mother gave birth in the family apartment. My grandmother served as the midwife for my birth and as my mother delivered me into this world, Grandma emptied a dresser drawer and placed it on the floor next to my mother's bed. That was my first crib. Thanks Grandma for the humble beginnings.

My life began in a very humble fashion indeed, born in a third-floor walkup apartment of a tenement building on 112th Street in Manhattan. Then and now, 112th Street is right in the middle of a ghetto, a community called Spanish Harlem. There were two apartments on each floor of our building. The apartments ran the length of the building, making the rooms line up in a row much like a bowling alley. Each apartment had a kitchen and an adjacent bathroom followed by four more rooms. Those rooms were used as family rooms and bedrooms.

New York City is famous for its many diverse neighborhoods such as Little Italy, Chinatown, SOHO (South of Houston Street – pronounced "house-ton" not like Houston, Texas). There's also Harlem, home of the famous Apollo Theater. The architecture is very much the same in each of these older communities, all turn-of-the-century tenement and brownstone buildings.

Life in Spanish Harlem in the 1950's had its moments of magic for kids. We played in the rubble of demolished buildings and inside the skeleton of burned-out warehouses and old theaters. We had our very own, make-believe, war zone. We'd play Ringo-leaveo (Tag, you're it!) for hours, hiding in the alleyways and rooftops of the tenements buildings. The tenement buildings were mostly five and six story structures grouped side-by-side. You could go from rooftop to rooftop around the entire block, unless there was a one-story warehouse in between the buildings or an empty lot; most often caused by a burned out building. We had multiple mountain top views to look out over the war zone.

You never really had to go down to the street to go visit a neighbor; you just used the rooftops. Those rooftops were the playgrounds of the teenaged kids while the streets and alleyways belonged to the younger kids. Rooftops were also the summer havens for those who couldn't get away to the beaches of Coney Island in Brooklyn or Orchard Beach in the Bronx.

Our view from the rooftops was of crowded streets; crowded with vendors pushing their carts full of everything from fruit to clothes, of cars of all vintages parked bumper to bumper, and of hundreds of people. You could see people of all ages sitting on the entryway steps, stoops, of their apartment buildings and telling stories. Kids would be playing stickball in the middle of the street while others ate snow cones purchased from a street vendor pushing a cart loaded with a huge block of ice. The vendor would shave the ice and let you select from one of the fifteen varieties of flavored syrups neatly lined-up around the block of ice.

The sounds of music were everywhere and they only came in one language, Spanish, and in one rhythm, Caribbean. The soft, romantic voices of El Trio De Los Panchos, Vicentico Valdez, and Tito Rodriquez would quiet the streets. When you heard the timbale and conga beats of the great Tito Puente, Mongo Santamaria, Joe Cuba, and Johnny Pacheco you had no choice but to dance, dance, and dance some more. The music came from the windows of just about every apartment, candy-store, and bar on the block. Everyone, young and old alike, identified with the music; it was in our blood.

The sounds never changed. They remained unique to our piece of Manhattan. It didn't matter if we were marching behind a hearse on its way to a funeral parlor, behind the tall religious statues carried high above the ground by the older men in a church ceremony, or just strolling along in the Puerto Rican Day Parade, the sounds and the rhythm remained the same, Caribbean.

There was also a very strong sense of community within our small piece of Manhattan. I can honestly say that in all my travels around the world, I've never experienced a greater sense of community than I did in Spanish Harlem as a boy. Sure, we were poor, but you wouldn't know it by the richness of our culture, the generosity of the people, and the sense of hope our elders had for us kids.

Three languages were heard throughout Spanish Harlem above all the other street noise: Spanish, English, and Spanglish. The elders spoke only Spanish, while the young adults and kids spoke English amongst themselves but a mix of Spanish and English – Spanglish, to the elders.

Our home was filled with three generations, my grandmother, my mother and her four sons, Raphael, Michael, Victor, and me. My mother's sister, Maria Dolores lived with us along with my grandmother's niece, Aida Luz, a total of four women and four boys. Notice I didn't mention my father. That's because all I have are just a few brief memories of him from the time I was about five years old.

I doubt that any of us kids living in Spanish Harlem back in the 1950s understood or would've given a rat's ass about socioeconomic comparisons. I don't remember identifying the word ghetto with my neighborhood until I was about ten or twelve. All the Latino kids I knew throughout New York knew my neighborhood as El Barrio, Spanish words for a precinct, district, or quarter, as in Spanish Quarter. There was no identity with being at the lower end of the socioeconomic ladder. El Barrio was, and in many ways remains just a neighborhood.

Don't get me wrong, I wasn't unhappy. What did I know then, I was just a child. Sure, I often wondered why some neighborhoods looked cleaner, pristine compared to my neighborhood. So what difference does that makes? Ghetto was a good word, wasn't it? We didn't have door attendants at the entrance to our apartment buildings, nor were our streets tree-lined boulevards leading to big botanical gardens where one could bond with Mother Nature. Again, so what?

My part of the city didn't have mega-supermarkets like the ones created in the 1990s. However, we could claim to have had one of the first covered malls, an enclosed shopping center under the elevated tracks of the Pennsylvania Railroad. The market, often referred to as La Marqueta (a convoluted Spanglish word for market), was the center of commerce, six city blocks of small vendors selling everything from meat to shoes, and suits to peaches. We also had Mom and Pop bodegas, candy stores and street vendors selling Coconut Ices, fresh fruits, and vegetables from their pushcarts. We had streets filled with people, singing, dancing, and playing dominoes all day long.

If the summer heat got to us and our parents were away at work, taking a trip to the beach was out of the question. We usually solved that problem by just opening the nearest fire hydrant and creating our own ocean spray. Any street-smart kid could open a fire hydrant with a wire hanger and a small stick. Then all you had to do was cut both ends of a tin can and you had a high-speed water nozzle. We entertained ourselves as well as all the folks who watched the world go by from the windows of their apartments.

Let me ask you, with all those distractions, did I really need to see what was on the other side of the tracks? There's a certain amount of truth in the saying, "If you've never had it, you'll never miss it!"

Having been born in Spanish Harlem and sharing a three-bedroom apartment four floors above the noisy streets with seven other women and children, I really didn't miss much as a child. My world and the world of everyone around me was full, not of wonder but of down-to-earth realities. You knew you were poor only because everyone else said you were. You measured your poverty against your neighbors' and you counted your blessings when you fooled yourself into thinking that you were better off than the family on the second floor.

The Barrio community, though seemingly poor, thrived. Many households were not only composed of mothers, fathers, sisters and brothers; but of aunts, uncles, cousins and often, grandparents too. Everyone who could work did so. The workers would pool portions of their incomes in a family savings plan. The Doña of the house often maintained those meager family accounts.

Multiple generations within one household, pooling their resources for a self-determined period, was the economic recipe for survival and success of most immigrant families throughout the twentieth century. Those pooled resources would eventually be shared by the entire family as the means of creating businesses, buying homes, and providing quality education for the young. Most Puerto Rican families followed that recipe.

One Hundred Twelfth Street, between Park and Madison Avenues, was home to my family and my friends. That small piece of Manhattan was friendly and at the same time, quite hostile. If you didn't belong there, you were best advised to stay out. Puertorriqueños are people of passion. Such passion was exhibited openly in El Barrio.

The passion was gentle, soft-spoken, and deep in the character of the "Boricua." Boricua is derived from Boriquén, the name given the island by the Taínos, the indigenous people enslaved by Spain.

While gentle, the Boricua passion very often spawned jealous rage, machismo, independence, and pride. You needed to understand that passion if you wanted to walk the streets of Spanish Harlem safely. Those streets were tough then and still are.

El Barrio was a very sheltered and somewhat exclusive community throughout the late forties and remains very much the same today. It had no true boundaries in its early years, more like buffer zones, racially mixed areas. Madison to Fifth Avenues on the West, 116th to 125th Street on the North, 98th to 100th Street on the South, and 2nd to 3rd Avenue on the East were the buffer zones. This chosen concentration of the Caribbean world was surrounded by a mixed group of similarly concentrated communities of Americans whose ancestries are from throughout Africa, Asia, Europe, and the Middle East. Each community had its own flavor and smell, along with its own way of walking, talking, and surviving.

The beauty of El Barrio would come out in moments of joy, sadness, success, and failure. Births and birthdays; christenings and first communions; engagements and weddings were all grand events filled with music, food and lots of friends and family.

Weddings were the grandest of all events in Spanish Harlem. Most wedding receptions were held in apartments. Can you imagine hosting one hundred people in a small apartment? The crowds often overflowed into the building's hallways and front steps. If you weren't inside the apartment dancing, drinking or eating, chances were you were outside on the sidewalk, dancing, drinking, or eating. Hors d'oeuvres were never on the menu of a Puerto Rican wedding reception in Spanish Harlem. No way! You ate traditional foods; rice, beans, pernil (roast pork), arroz con pollo (rice with chicken), fried fish, tostónes (fried plantains), and some of the best wedding cake I've ever tasted from the Valencia Bakery in the middle of Spanish Harlem.

Illness and death were celebrated throughout Spanish Harlem as well. No family was left to suffer any pains alone. Neighbors became family and clung to each other. A classmate of mine died from leukemia when he was ten years old. I remember my aunt, Maria Dolores, taking me to the boy's home to comfort his family and pray with them. When the father of our next-door neighbor died, the women of the neighborhood brought food to my neighbor's house for two months. The men of the neighborhood pooled their money and paid for the family's expenses, including their rent so they wouldn't be moved out of the neighborhood. Honor was paid to the deceased and their family with a procession of neighbors, men, women and children, who followed the hearse from the funeral parlor to the local church. El Barrio may have been "badlands" to outsiders but it was a marvelous place to me.

The parties at my house were always special. It's somewhat odd, yet heartwarming, that some of my most vivid recollections of my grandmother occur during the Feast of the Three Kings – a party.

The Epiphany, as it's known throughout the Christian world, celebrates the story of when three kings named Melchor, Baltazar, and Gaspar visited the Christ child in Bethlehem. In Puerto Rico, as in many Latin countries, December 25 is recognized as the birth date of Jesus Christ. The day is filled with solemn, religious ceremonies. The gift giving and revelry of the Christmas season is reserved for January 6, the Epiphany.

I clearly recall those first Christmas holidays. The tree would be set up in the living room and a manger, with its ceramic figurines, would be placed under the tree. Mysteriously or miraculously, different animals would show up under the tree as December 25 drew closer. There would be cows, goats, camels, and mules all placed in position by something or someone each night. On the morning of December 25, Joseph, Mary and the Christ child would be in place. There would also be some small, token gifts under the tree for each of us in the house. On the other side of the room, three ceramic kings on camelback, along with their entourage of servants and caretakers, would appear on the floor.

The figurines would move closer to the manger daily. It was obvious to me, as a child, that some powerful force was moving the kings toward the manger. No doubt that between December 25 and January 6 the kings would be under foot but great care would be taken not to disturb their journey. As planned, the Three Kings arrived at the manger on the morning of January 6. That's when the real celebration of the Christmas season would begin.

The observance of the Feast of the Three Kings was something very dear to my grandmother. She made sure that if she were to bring only one tradition to New York, one glimpse of her Old World customs; it would certainly be this celebration. Year after year, I would hear the elders relive the sweet memories of how they celebrated La Fiesta de Los Reyes in Puerto Rico.

Stories told of how the fiesta would begin in the valleys of Yabucoa and how the family would gather their children and friends and travel from house to house bringing with them simple delicacies made just for the feast. They would roast a pig over an open fire and cut it in quarters in order to make it easy to carry. Large caldrons of rice, red beans, and fried plantains would also be brought along, always more than enough to feed everyone.

The food and the children would be placed into horse drawn carts and the group would go from house to house sharing their food, spreading joy, and praising the Three Kings discovery of the Christ Child. The celebration would be taken into the hills; no one was ever denied a visit. If you were sick and unable to come to the fiesta, the fiesta came to you. When you got tired, you slept, and when you woke up, you went back to the party. This was a celebration of life and of family. All ill feelings were forgotten, only love filled the air.

That's exactly the way it was in New York City. My grandmother, just like many of the other abuelitas in El Barrio, would begin planning for the feast months in advance. She would start preparing her special delicacies in mid-December. Time had to be allowed for such things as Coquíto, Puerto Rican eggnog, to age properly and be perfect for the fiesta. My grandmother would enlist the help of several neighbors, specifically their kitchens, in order to prepare the food. The roast pig alone required four ovens. The other essentials would be prepared and cooked on the day of the feast over many stoves within the tenement building.

The religious meaning of the day was never lost. Before one drink was served or one meal eaten that evening, the guest would gather in a specially prepared room and say the rosary. The manger would have already been removed from under the tree and placed on a small table where a tiny piece of incense would be burning. Behind the manger would be a sheet of white linen hanging on the wall. Guest would pin donations on the sheet as they entered the room. My eyes would gaze over the $5, $10, and $20 dollar bills that would cover the sheet before the evening ended. My grandmother would kneel during the entire rosary, quietly praying and reciting her responses as the rosary was said. Her sister, Virginia, would always lead the rosary. For that matter, Aunt Virginia led every rosary that was ever recited in our house. The money would later be collected and taken to the parish church as an offering to the Christ Child. Once the rosary was completed, the celebration began.

All those preparations of food and gatherings of family and friends seemed easy enough when the family was in Puerto Rico. However, this was New York City in the early fifties, in particular, Spanish Harlem. The automobile replaced the horse drawn carts. I remember piling into a car with as many as twelve to fourteen men, women, and children – talk about mass transportation!

At every stop we made, my grandmother with a guitar in hand, would lead the crowd in Aguinaldos, Spanish Christmas carols, as her Christmas gifts to those inside the home. When the occupants of the apartment opened their door, they too would join in the singing.

Grandma would then enter the home, light some incense, and bless the home and everyone in it. Neighbors, who could not help but hear the joyful noise made by the group, would open their doors too and sing along. They would also be welcomed to join the family and feast with us on the food and drink we had brought along with us. Apartment to apartment, through all parts of El Barrio, Grandma would lead her procession in celebration of the Three Kings' visit to the Christ Child.

The last Fiesta de Los Reyes, hosted by my grandmother, was in January 1964. That celebration ended with a visit to the home of my Uncle Salvador and Aunt Aida in Bayport, Long Island, some sixty-five miles from New York City. Uncle Salvador and his family were unable to travel into the city and enjoy the fiesta with the rest of the family. Grandma, however, was determined that the entire family would be together.

The day of that last feast had begun in the same manner, as had all the others: food was being prepared, last minute guests were being invited, the apartment was being cleaned meticulously, and the children were required to be available for quick trips to the market. Little did anyone know that Grandma had already set plans in motion for the trip to Bayport. No one had noticed the extra portions of food that had been prepared. Everyone had simply suspected that a larger than normal group had been invited.

Later in the evening, my grandmother announced to everyone that the family was leaving the city and taking the celebration to Salvador's house; everyone was welcomed to join us. We packed all the food and drink we could, along with suitcases stuffed with enough clothes for a few days into a van, and then we crammed ourselves into two cars. The ride would take ninety minutes. Fourteen adults and children descended on a quiet neighborhood in Bayport at 11:30PM.

True to our family's customs and traditions, my grandmother rang the doorbell and immediately started to sing. We all joined her in song as she delivered her son and his family their Aguinaldos. I remember the look on the faces of my uncle and aunt, surprise, joy, tears and laughter. Our singing woke up the neighbors and soon many of them joined us for a nightlong celebration. That last Feast of the Three Kings lasted three days.

There are other prized memories of my childhood that come to mind very easily. Some of the most wonderful moments I remember took place along the shores of Coney Island in New York City. The trip to the beach was always a Saturday morning family ritual during the hot and humid summer months. I never failed to get up early on those Saturdays; the smell of the fried chicken my mother prepared for the picnic basket always filled the air. Her menu never changed; fried chicken, potato salad, peaches, bananas, plums, and soft drinks.

I vividly recall two of my favorite rides, the Cyclone and the Bobsled. Better yet, the Parachute, the giant Merry-Go-Round and the wooden horses on the steel tracks of the Steeplechase, were all great rides from the early days of Coney Island. I can still taste the salty corn-on-the-cob and the greasy french-fries served in the same style of paper cups used for our icy snow cones. Oddly enough, the feel of the wooden planks that made the diagonal pattern on the boardwalk and the searing, burning white sand under my feet are always welcomed memories; outdone only by the feel of the cool sand at the water's edge.

I often wished I were one of those kids who lived in the bungalows that lined the boulevards near the shore. I had to take a one-hour subway ride from the inner city to reach Coney Island; but they were right there! Those kids lived in little homes with flower gardens, striped awnings, patio furniture, and big sedans parked on the clean streets in front of each house. Living close to the beach; a great place for a kid to have wonderful daydreams. Daydreams were private places where you could invite imaginary friends from across the ocean into your own make-believe world.

I really didn't feel a strong sense of envy for those beach kids though. I too shared loads of fun, laughter, and love with my family at Coney Island. Truthfully, what I looked forward to most throughout the year was standing alone at the water's edge.

I can't recall exactly how old I was when it happened; but I can clearly picture a very special moment at the beach in my mind's eye. I couldn't have been more than eight or nine years old when I stood on the shore at Coney Island, feeling as if I had the beach all to myself. I remember looking out over the ocean and wondering what the significance of the horizon was. I remember seeing a few tugboats and a couple of freighters that were well off shore; but just like the people around me, they really didn't draw my attention. I was interested in the horizon.

Exactly what was beyond that thin seam that separated the water from the sky, the heavens from the earth? That question and the pursuit of its many answers marked a turning point in my life. I was just a kid filled with lots of questions about things that were truly unknowns to me, truly alien. I found myself daydreaming of what could be beyond that horizon. I'm sure that everything I had dreamed about, prior to that wondrous moment, was of things I knew: my school, my family, the market under the elevated train tracks that made its own seam right down the middle of Spanish Harlem. Sure, I could add some of the stuff I saw on TV shows like Howdy Doody, the Lone Ranger, Sky King, Spanky and the Gang or the Bowery Boys to my daydreams; but those were known things and that wasn't the same as those unknowns beyond that horizon.

Yes, there were many wondrous moments in Spanish Harlem. Unfortunately, an inner-city kid's life is often a never-ending series of shocking revelations. As an eight-year old kid in New York City, I had already been exposed to sex, violence, broken homes, adultery, unwed mothers and their fatherless children, alcoholism and the resulting jobless drunks sitting out their days on the steps of their apartment buildings. I need you to note that I said, "Exposed." That's an important note to keep in mind. I was a young kid and it didn't matter what or how much I was exposed to, I didn't necessarily understand or accept any of it.

In my mind's eye, it was always sunny and warm over the horizon and there were always many things to do. The streets were clean and tree-lined. Moreover, there were big, grassy parks there where we could go fly kites and play baseball. There were no harsh words spoken. My mother and I would be happier there.

Nothing was impossible or improbable in the childlike fantasies I created every time I went to the beach and let my mind wander past the horizon. All of Mother Nature's glory, exciting adventures, and rewarding opportunities were just over that edge of the world. If I could just get over there, I could be someone else, do something else, and know newer things.

Those were the thoughts of a young boy. Would knowing, understanding and appreciating the details of my grandmother's journey over her "edge of the world" have helped me with my view of what was possible? I believe it would have. Just as I believe that if you take a little bit of time to study your family's history, you too will see the endless possibilities that exist for you.

"Never be bullied into silence. Never allow yourself to be made a victim. Accept no one's definition of your life; define yourself."

Harvey Fierstein

Chapter Four
Street Smarts

Spanish Harlem was a predominantly Roman Catholic community when I was a kid and many of my friends attended the parochial schools that surrounded that area of New York City. Michael and I went to Commander John J. Shea Memorial School on 111th Street between Lexington and Park Avenues in Manhattan. Commander Shea, a U.S. Navy officer, was killed during a World War II battle against the Japanese Imperial Navy far away in the South Pacific. I found it curious and intriguing attending a Catholic school whose name memorialized a war hero; Catholic schools were usually named after a saint or patron of the church.

The school was a big stone and brick building with a large chapel and a gym inside the building. It was one of the older, institutional buildings in the neighborhood. Long before 111th Street was in the middle of Spanish Harlem, it was in the middle of a Jewish ghetto. The building was a Jewish school and synagogue – a unique transition, from the Star of David to a Crucifix.

As a kid, I could only identify with life within my world. That single-minded view really influenced me when I ventured outside of my neighborhood into other parts of the city. Whenever I went outside the borders of Spanish Harlem, I felt as if I were in another reality. The music was different, jazz and soul in the African American Harlem, classical on Fifth Avenue, and tenors singing arias in Little Italy. The neighborhoods were different, but a good different.

One thing for sure, I didn't want to stand out in any of those other neighborhoods where I often felt out of place. Something inside me kept telling me, "Hey Joe, you don't belong here." Sometimes it came to me as a warning, while at other times it came just as a fact of status. Rich people, people of means, lived along Fifth Avenue and Central Park. I was a kid from Spanish Harlem. My park didn't have trees.

My park was 112th Street. Its black asphalt was our chalkboard where we lined-out our infield for stickball, the triangle for hopscotch, and our giant checkerboards, each drawn with colorful chalk. The rooftops of the tenement buildings were our private hangouts where we held our gang meetings, shared secrets, and plotted our retaliation against the kids from 113th Street. I knew every alleyway, every shortcut and escape route in Spanish Harlem that would get me back to 112th Street safely. Maybe it was instinct, but I knew where I was most comfortable. Maybe you could say it's where I really belonged.

Michael is one year and eleven days older than I am and, like most kids, he went to kindergarten when he was five years old. However, when I turned five and was supposed to start kindergarten, I insisted on going to class with my brother. Apparently, I made such a scene on my first day of kindergarten that the nuns from the Sisters of Mercy Order, who taught at the school, decided to put me in the first grade along with Michael. I was allowed to stay as long as I could keep up with the schoolwork the first-graders were doing. Michael and I became the "Salt and Pepper" twins – two Aliceas in the same classroom. That was the beginning of a great brotherhood – Michael and me.

Right about the time we entered the fifth grade, our family moved us out of Spanish Harlem to a more interracially mixed neighborhood on 98th Street and Lexington Avenue. Instead of walking to school, Michael and I rode a city bus for the fifteen-minute ride to 111th Street. Ninety-Eight Street was a neat neighborhood where kids of all colors just hung out together playing all the street games, tag, checkers, and stickball. We did our best inventing as many ways as possible to have fun.

Toy dealers in America introduced a series of high-tech, two-wheeled scooters in the fall of 2000. Kids, everywhere, received those chrome beauties at Christmas time. Well here's some news for you – we had scooters in the 1950s too. Our scooters weren't lightweight or chrome-plated and they didn't have high-tech plastic wheels either. Our store-bought scooters were made of galvanized steel painted fire engine red and had rubber wheels.

All the kids in my neighborhood had scooters. If you were too poor to buy one, you could easily make one out of a single roller skate, a four-foot section of 2X4 lumber, a wooden milk crate, and a few nails. Back then, roller skates were made of steel; steel wheels and a two-part frame that you clamped onto your shoes (you might want to ask your parents or grandparents about those steel skates and the special skate key).

Building a scooter was simple; you nailed half of the skate and the milk crate to the one end of the 2X4 and the other half of the skate to the other end. If you had style, you'd put handlebars on the milk crate and nailed tin cans on the front of the crate as make-believe headlights. The cooler kids would just nail the two parts of the skate to the 2X4 and propel themselves down the street; much like today's skateboards. That's right; we had skateboards before you did, and they were really cool!

There was no sense envying anyone with money. You just had to make do with what you had. You had to be creative and innovative, and if that failed, you always had your imagination. Poor kids dream a great deal; I know I did.

Something hit me early in life, the reality that money buys things. If you wanted things as a kid, you asked your parents. "We'll see," "Maybe," or the all-time favorite "Ask Santa Claus," was the answer my mother gave to most of my requests. I just had to find another way of getting things. Dreams didn't hack it, so I went to work.

I started my first job when I was nine years old. A few kids from my block came up with the idea of building shoeshine boxes, hustling some of the older guys around the neighborhood, and making some money. Shining shoes? How degrading! Well it wasn't to me. I felt that it was a different way of hanging out with some of my pals, walk around the neighborhood, and maybe make a few bucks.

My mother, however, felt that shining shoes was indeed degrading, well beneath us. Our family didn't shine other people's shoes. I guess that in her mind we weren't poor enough to shine shoes. I never thought about it like that then or now.

After just a few days into my first career, I figured out where the bucks were – the neighborhood bars. At nine, I was a little snot of a kid and I used my lack of height to my advantage. I'd walk into a neighborhood bar and work my way through the crowds carrying my handmade shoeshine box. Then I'd just walk up to potential customers and ask if they would like me to make their shoes look nicer. The bars' customers, mostly men, rarely said no to a little kid; especially a kid carrying a heavy box full of brushes, rags, and waxes.

I quickly learned how to work the crowds. I rarely approached a man sitting at the bar by himself; he didn't have anyone to impress. However, when I saw a group of men standing at the bar together, I could smell the money. I'd slip in between the men, pick one of them out, and ask, "Hey Mister, those are nice shoes. May I shine 'em up for you?" My target would look around to the other men in the group, his chest would puff up, and he'd grab his waistband and adjust his pants. Looking like a cool dude, a tough person, or a high roller kind of guy, my target would say, "Yeah, sure kid."

Home Run! I had him. Then I'd do my stuff – two brushes, working simultaneously, cleaning the dust off his shoes. Next came some liquid cleaner, and lots of shoe wax. I was always careful with the sock, and paid extra attention to the welt, sole, and heel. I would finish with some more brushwork and lots of snappin' and poppin' of the shoe rag – nothing but showmanship!

I never looked up from the man's shoes until I was done. I just did my stuff and listened carefully to their conversations, never giving them a hint that I was eavesdropping. If they stopped talking while I did my show stuff or if they were saying anything about me, I'd just press on and do the best job I could. When I finished, I would stand up and ask my customer, "Is that OK Mister?"

"That's great kid! What do I owe you?" the customer usually said.

I always replied, "Only twenty-five cents, Sir. That's all I charge." That's when peer pressure took over. My customer would look at his friends and he usually pulled out a couple of bucks. He wanted to impress his friends. Two or more of the other men in the group would then ask me to shine their shoes too and they always paid me the same, if not more, than the first guy did. Peer pressure – something that had a greater meaning as I got older. I got more than just money shining shoes in NYC bars. I got an education too.

What could a nine-year old kid possibly learn while shining shoes in a bar that was of any value? Often times, men would just carry on with their conversation as if I, a kid, wasn't in the room. They spoke about women, the ones they loved, and the ones they wanted to love. They bragged about sex in vulgar terms. Sometimes they helped each other with teaching words. The men also spoke about their jobs, their bosses, new jobs they were looking for, and old ones they hated. They even spoke of new ways of doing business and what future technology they had read about in magazines or heard about on the radio. Could the technology work? Would their jobs be in jeopardy? Was it all science fiction?

When those grownup guys at the bars spoke of the women in their lives, the women fit into four categories: She's the one for me; She might be the one for me; She's not the one for me; She's OK for now. Let me ask you, what's a little snot of a kid supposed to do with those pearls of wisdom? I tried my best not to place too much value on anything my customers spoke about; however, their words about women in the first category – She's the one for me – always caught my attention.

The words I heard and understood from those bar room conversations went beyond the "nice person; pretty face; good family; fine cook," identification. The words that stuck with me were, "She knows how to take care of me; she's good to me; I really like being with her." I was a kid but those words made sense to me.

The vulgar words about sex were words I knew my grandmother wouldn't have appreciated me hearing. However, I heard them anyway and probably too often on the streets of the city, especially in the bars. I remember wondering what had made the men that used those words so angry as to speak of women in those vulgar terms. Frankly, I still don't understand it. If you feel badly about someone, just get that person out of your life.

Sure, I heard plenty of vulgar words but I really listened to the teaching words – men sharing with other men, usually one-on-one, not in groups, words that spoke of how you should treat a woman. Those conversations weren't just about physical sex. I listened to men talk about taking their ladies out to dinner, a Broadway show, or a movie. Flowers, candy, jewelry, clothes, money – things they gave to please that special lady in their life. Boat rides, picnics in the park, long car rides in the countryside – things they did to show their lady how much they wanted to be with her.

I often heard the men agree on one thing when it came to women; you didn't cheat on your main squeeze. If you did and were busted, you deserved it. If you cheated and she walked out on you, you deserved that too. If you cheated on her and she came to the bar with a knife or a gun, you screwed up BIG time and your friends didn't want you to come back to that bar.

Having shined a few pairs of shoes, I never left a bar without hearing one of the men tell another, "That kid's going to do OK." I was often told, "It's OK to start at the bottom and work your way up kid." It didn't take too long to figure out what those words meant. What struck me then as amazing was how easy it was to make money. The harder I worked at shining shoes, the more business I got. "Good Work + More Business = More Money," an easy equation for a nine year old to figure out.

When those men spoke about their jobs, many of them moaned and groaned about working too hard or about long hours and low pay. But a few of them talked about learning new skills, going back to school, and making themselves better in order to compete for higher paying jobs. Moaning and groaning didn't hack it! "You learn = you earn," another simple equation. Somehow, I knew that down the road of my life I would have to use some of those pearls of wisdom I picked up during my days of shining shoes.

If you're wondering, what I did with all the money I made at my first job, the answer is simple; I gave all of it to my mother. She needed the money more than I did; fifty dollars could easily feed a small family for one week in the 1950's. Hey, what was I going to do with the $30 - $50 dollars I earned every Friday, Saturday, or Sunday working the bars from 98th to 86th Street along Lexington and Third Avenues of Manhattan? Yes, it was a lot of work, but I had a lot of fun doing it and the education was priceless.

By the time I started high school, I had worked many different jobs. I knew how to fix flat tires, pump gas, and change the motor oil of a car. I also worked part-time after school at hamburger joints flipping burgers and as a messenger in downtown Manhattan, delivering letters and small packages.

There were two jobs I enjoyed the most as a kid. One was working at a candy store selling newspapers, making ice cream sundaes, and egg-cream sodas (that's a NYC thing). The other was working at a Carvel Ice Cream franchise creating all sorts of ice cream delights. What I liked about those jobs was the face-to-face

49

contact I had with the customers. Both jobs afforded me the opportunity to speak to all sorts of people: young, old, of different races, and speaking many languages. Most importantly, for me as a young kid, was the chance to meet girls, lots of girls.

By the way, in case you're wondering what I did with the money I earned while in high school; I paid my own way. I paid for my own clothes, movies, bowling, baseball games, dates, and all the other hanging-out-on-the-streets stuff I did. I tried my best to lighten my mother's load.

"An insincere and evil friend is more to be feared than
a wild beast; a wild beast may wound your body, but
an evil friend will wound your mind."

Buddha

Chapter Five
A Tidal Wave of Drugs

Up to a certain point in my life, I really hadn't paid much
attention to the vices of adults. At the age of five, I already knew that
alcohol and alcoholism could destroy individuals and families. I had
already been exposed to adultery too. I didn't understand it beyond
the scope of my father cheating on my mother with another woman.
Something had to be wrong considering my mom and dad were very
mad and very sad too. Truthfully, as a kid caught up in that mess, I
couldn't figure out if the wrong part of my parents' marriage was the
fact that Dad cheated on Mom or that he did it in the neighborhood. I
didn't know yet what that "it" was but hey, I was only five years old
and growing fast.

I was about nine years old when my mother moved us to 98th
Street and Lexington Avenue. The neighborhood was a rainbow blend
of nationalities, including a good mix of Latino families. We lived
there for about two and one-half years and it was during that brief

period that I first witnessed one of America's greatest tragedies –
Drug Abuse.

The absolute weirdest thing to me was seeing the older kids
fooling around with drugs. Imagine being nine or ten years old and
actually watching teenagers pumping heroin into their veins. The
more drugs they took, the weirder they became. I couldn't understand
the attraction to drugs when all these teenagers ended up doing while
they were drugged was walking around like a bunch of zombies. Kids
my age just tried to ignore the junkies as they stood on street corners,
hunched over in a stupor, talking gibberish. If that's what taking drugs
was all about – No Thank You!

How the junk got into our neighborhood was something I
didn't think of questioning. All I can remember was that it came like a
fast thunderstorm and flooded the area, striking the fifteen through
nineteen-year-old kids in the neighborhood. Suddenly, I found myself
walking around increasing numbers of young guys and gals standing
stupefied at the corners of my block as I learned new words like
Smack, Nickel Bag and Stone-Cold Junkie. By the time I was ten, I
really started wondering what was attracting so many kids to drugs.
The answers to all my questions came sooner than expected,
remember, I said I was growing fast.

To this day, I can still recall the name of one of the prettiest
girls from 98th Street, a girl who went by the nickname of Blackie. I
may have been ten years old at the time, but I knew a good-looking
girl when I saw one. Blackie was a tall, fair-skinned, brown-haired
teenager who treated all the kids as if she were our big sister. She

would sing songs and read books to us. She enjoyed helping the young girls comb their hair and dress up their dolls. She even helped me with a couple of model airplanes I built.

Blackie only wore a little bit of make-up, always had her hair combed really pretty, and her perfume was nothing like what my mother or grandmother wore. I'm sure I had as big a crush on her as all the other guys I hung out with did. Sadly, it wasn't long after I began to know Blackie that the wave of drugs hit 98th Street. That same wave slammed into Blackie's life and she soon became a Stone-Cold Junkie.

Blackie's transformation from friendly sister to spaced-out stranger was almost overnight. I remember seeing her standing in the doorway of my apartment building shortly after the flood of drugs had caught up with her. I had never seen her like that before. She was wearing a wrinkled and dirty white blouse and a pair of tight, black mini pants (very short, shorts). Her eyes were sunken and dark and her skin was ashen. She greeted me in her usual style but her words were slurred and broken. The smile on her face, that smile that had often greeted me so warmly, looked as though it took a great deal of effort for her to create. The smell of her silky perfume was gone.

Blackie reached out and hugged me and I hugged her back. I asked her what was wrong. She said, "Nothing sweetie, I'm just a little high." High? What a strange word to use for something that clearly put her down. I was confused. "High" was just another word for me to decode and understand.

I'm sorry to say that I never learned Blackie's real name. The memories of watching her life, along with the lives of so many of the other young men and women from the block, fade away under the influence of drugs still saddens me and fills me with questions. What was it about heroin that was so delicious, so inviting, and so necessary that they would give up their future for this "High"?

A short while after Blackie and so many other neighborhood kids turned to drugs, my mother decided to move to another part of the city. This time we left Manhattan and moved to the Bronx. One of New York City's five boroughs, the Bronx was just an extension of Manhattan, a little bit of suburb and heaps of urban crowding. It wasn't 98th Street, but Eagle Avenue in the South Bronx wouldn't win any prizes either.

While I may not have known Blackie's real name, I did know the name of another kid whose life fell apart because of drugs. His name was Ralph. I knew him and his family. Ralph was a quiet kid who made average grades in school but he had a special gift. He could see music. He had learned to play the piano early in his life and by the time he was twelve years old he was already playing at several concert halls in New York City.

Music meant fun to Ralph. He enjoyed playing for his family and for their friends. Most of all, Ralph enjoyed playing for the neighborhood kids who would come to his family's apartment and ask if he'd play a little bit for them. He would play more than just a little bit. The kids didn't know it but they were being exposed to classical, jazz, and pop music; all were Ralph's favorites.

I was one of those kids who would listen to Ralph play for hours on end. During the school week, I would rush to do my homework and then wait for Ralph to get home. He would practice for at least one-hour right after he got home from school. On weekends, his music filled the neighborhood all day. Little did I know that those long hours at the keyboard, seeking perfection, were not Ralph's choice but his mother's demands.

My family had moved from a fifth-floor walk-up in Manhattan to a three-story complex in the Bronx. The sun seemed brighter there. Kids played in the street all day long while the elderly folks sat on milk crates lined up along the front of the apartment buildings, gossiping and enjoying the sun's warmth. Young mothers would stroll up the avenue with their baby's carriages and stop to speak to those elderly folks. The elders were always eager to share stories of their days as young parents. There were gardeners who spruced-up their backyards on Saturdays and churchgoers who got all dressed-up on Sundays.

Life in the South Bronx seemed good and it had a sense of promise, at least until the flood of drugs reached out and crushed the South Bronx too. Drugs touched every family I knew. It touched Ralph's family deeply. Drugs stimulated, captured, and eventually destroyed most of its captives. I watched it destroy Ralph.

From a gifted pianist, artist, writer, and loving son, I saw drugs turn Ralph into a thief and a liar. He stole from his friends and family. Jewelry, furniture, appliances, money, and clothes were his barter to support that monkey on his back. He forgot the piano, he dropped out of school, and he even tried marriage; sadly that failed within months of leaving the altar. His life became an endless series of failed recoveries and jail time, promises to his mother and heartbreak to his grandmother.

As the years passed, Ralph's body became a shell whose organs eventually attacked him just as ruthlessly as the heroin he pumped into his veins. His body became a hollow shell that could barely stand up. A once gifted mind that commanded magical fingers became a mind requiring medication to curb depression and prevent strokes. His brain was fried!

Ralph was lost to drugs. Moreover, he has been lost to me for the last forty years. I must confess to you that Ralph is my oldest brother and I doubt that we've shared more than 100 words in these past 40 years. Drugs – they took my brother and stole his beautiful music.

I was the one who proudly brought the neighborhood kids home to listen to my brother play the piano. It didn't matter if Ralph played classical or jazz because we didn't care; it was just good music. Did the music attract us or was it simply being in the presence of someone from our neighborhood that could play the piano just like the people you saw on TV? It was both! We were in awe of his gifted hands as they danced over the piano keys. I miss his music. I deeply miss what his music could have been. I wonder if, in the darkness of his drug-destroyed mind and body, he misses what he could have been.

I wonder how many times he's damned that moment in his life when he chose the wrong path. Does he ask himself what his life could've, would've and should've been had he not taken that step? Moreover, I wonder how many regrets my mother has repeated in her mind and what scars those thoughts have left on her heart. That magical high from drugs destroys life. I witnessed that destruction and it opened my eyes. I've never walked down Ralph's path. I've never done drugs!

I'm sitting in the First Class section of American Airlines Flight 1587, Miami, Florida to Dallas, Texas and as I write this chapter, I'm forced to think of Ralph and the years he's wasted behind bars. I'm in a very comfortable seat in an airplane and he's in a crowded jail cell. My food is served on dinnerware, while his is served on plastic. I'm drinking wine from a glass and he's drinking water from a paper cup. I wouldn't trade places with Ralph, even if I could. He picked his bed, now he has to sleep in it.

I miss him a great deal; however, I especially miss what could have become of our brotherhood. The love we should have shared as brothers and the love he would have shared with my kids and grandkids. I sadly miss what could have been of his music. It's all gone. It will never be.

The flood of drugs hadn't receded by the time I reached my teenage years. On the contrary, it had already washed over every street in the city in an endless series of waves. It seemed as though everybody I knew was aware of, if not already doing drugs.

Most of the kids I hung out with were smoking pot. We even nicknamed some of the people "chimneys" – they were always SMOKIN'. Everybody talked about getting high and being cool. If you upset anyone while he or she was high, you would be labeled a "head-blower" because you messed up someone's high. That's right, we had our own set of words to learn like Reefer, Joint, and Roach.

Unlike the heroin addicts of the 1950's, the Potheads of the 1960's were in a different place, a different orbit, and a different high. Yet, the chimneys I knew made the same claims as the heroin addicts – "I can control my habit!" Nevertheless, all I saw them do was get deeper and deeper into drugs.

"But these are my friends," I would argue. When you hang with your peers you have to be into what they do, don't you? No, I didn't!

Yes, turning my back on drugs was tough; the peer pressure was constant. However, I had already seen where drugs could take someone and many of my friends were well on their way to that same place – Nowhere! In a matter of a few short years, I lost some of those friends. We split away from each other because their thing was not mine and as tempted, as I may have been to light up a joint and get high, I never made it my thing.

Does it sound like I was an outsider? Well I wasn't. I had my own way of getting a buzz on. My way was booze, the Devil's Brew, Suds – Alcohol, the legal high.

My boys would be smokin' and I'd be drinkin'. I drank cheap wine, cheap beer and some of the cheapest whiskey available. I could swear to you that some of the cheap Scotch Whiskey that came in a dark green bottle was green when I drank it. I drank until I couldn't talk, walk, or stop throwing up. My friends were chimneys and I was a lush, drinking like a fish. I slugged down more booze than any pothead I knew could. Moreover, they were proud of me. Damn, that made me feel good!

My friends would often take bets with the older teenagers and challenge me to drink a quart of cold beer, non-stop. I never lost! Yes stupidity ruled – my taking pride in what a bunch of teenaged potheads thought about my drinking prowess. That was max stupidity.

We were sophomores and juniors in high school who became partying fools. We'd skip school and throw parties at our homes while our parents were at work. Pot, booze, rock-n-roll, and boys and girls all alone in a house with no adult supervision were the ingredients for trouble, definitely plenty of trouble.

Did we stop to think about the consequences of our actions? Hell no! Party on! That was the rule. We were indestructible. We were teenagers. Weren't we supposed to enjoy those years? Didn't all that noise we heard from our parents about "wasting our lives" go away when we reached our 20's and became adults? Hey, all the mistakes we made and all of the rules we broke would be forgotten

59

when we reached that magical adult age of 21, right? We were dreaming!

[Note: Later in the book, I'll tell you more about how my drinking came about. I just wanted you to think about how downright stupid I must have been just for the sake of wanting to hang out with what I called "friends."]

Unfortunately, within a few years, many of the neighborhood kids turned into serious drug addicts. They dropped out of school but graduated with honors from "Marijuana High School" to "Heroin, Acid, and Pill-Popping University." Many scientists will argue whether smoking marijuana necessarily leads to increased drug abuse. However, those scientists can't argue with the realities of life we found on 174th Street and Bryant Avenue in the Bronx during the early '60s.

My mother had moved us to 174th Street to escape the South Bronx's drug scene, only to find that just as many kids were taking a ride on the drug elevator in the North Bronx and the elevator only went down. Moreover, once you were down and out, your chances of getting up were slim to none.

Many of my teenage friends, just kids, were strung out on junk and thrown out from their homes. Kids without jobs, an education, support from family or friends, and nowhere to go because of their drug habits. These weren't dumb kids from poor or uncaring families. These guys and gals were tall, short, fat, skinny, pretty, not so pretty, blond, brunette, pimple faced, freckle faced, white, black and brown intelligent kids from loving, and church-going families. They were kids who were overcome by a disease.

Several of those kids didn't survive their teen years. Their life ended early, painfully and often tragically. Some hung on to life until they were in their 30's; grown men and women strung out and facing death. What drug overdoses didn't kill, other diseases did.

Bartolome and Eddie died. Doc fried his brain and he was eventually institutionalized. Morgan, Junior, Gladys, Bonnie, Mike, Jimmy J., Alicia and a few others managed to evade the drug wave, survive and get away from that bogus high and its deadly claims.

I think it was the pain we saw our friends suffer through that forced us to reflect for a minute and say, "Not me!" Then, when we witnessed the anguish their families suffered as they buried what was supposed to be their family's hope for the future, we knew the stupidity had to stop. Ironically, those deaths saved many of us.

Amazingly, the amount of stuff and confusion that comes at you today is worse than when I was a kid. Today, the TV shows are bold, more adult-like than family-oriented. Today, violence on TV and in the movies is often mirrored on the streets you believe are safe. Sadly, violence has also found its way into our schools; places we've always felt were safe havens for learning. Today, teenagers experiment with sex at an early age, just as much as when I was a teenager; but unlike my generation, an alarming number of young teenagers today are infected with Sexually Transmitted Diseases

(STD). Today, teenaged girls are having babies at an equally alarming rate – Babies having Babies!

Beyond the tragedy of STDs or pregnancies, you and all your friends, even those who don't live anywhere near a big city in the United States, may still be in danger; in danger of having your life turned upside down by the giant wave of drug use in our Country. Your life is just beginning; you're at the beginning of your book! All of those dangerous, tragic, hurtful, and destructive things are really happening. I wish I could say they weren't, but they are. Somehow, you have to survive it all.

Here's the truth that the streets taught me about booze and drugs. Everybody talks about the "high" they get from doing drugs and how "cool" they are when they've had a few drinks. What a load of crap! That high is nothing but your brain telling you that it's not functioning properly and that you're not dealing from a full deck. The cool feeling from booze is pretty much the same thing. Get drunk and you'll be Three-Sheets-to-the-Wind. That sailing expression really translates into going nowhere fast. Drugs or alcohol won't get you anywhere – period! I know, I've been there, done that – got nowhere! I urge you to walk away.

I guarantee you that neither drugs nor alcohol will make you smarter, prettier, handsomer, taller, shorter, wiser, gallant, sincere, attractive, richer, or any better than you are today. I've never known a junkie or a drunk to look at their reflection in a mirror; they wouldn't like what they saw. What makes you think anyone else will?

Anybody that tells you, "Try it, you'll like it; it won't hurt you; you won't get addicted to it; you can stop at anytime;" is a liar. Plainly and simply, that person is a damn liar! What's worst is that they don't care one iota about you, not a rat's ass about you, or your future. If you hear those "Try it, you'll like it" words, I suggest you walk away as fast as you can.

Who are the only people that want to get next to a junkie or a drunk? That's right, just junkies or drunks. You will only attract people who are like you. Don't expect that crowd you hang out with, the ones you call friends, to follow you down the rat hole that's at the end of the path you may have taken. Walking away from drugs is your best move.

Blackie was a point of reference for me when I first met her on 98th Street. She was someone I could look up to and say, "Wow! Isn't she great? She's going to be someone special." How about you taking a look around you, at those you've felt would become someone special; achieve great things; be successful. How would you feel if you saw them take a turn toward destruction and death the way I saw Blackie in the end? Would that make you think about how they got to such a low point? Would you want to follow their example or steer-clear of the path they took? I know that you have the answer – steer clear and walk away.

Do you remember the piece I wrote about Ralph? Well he just finished an eight-month stint in jail again. He pleaded innocent to the charges; but how innocent can an ex-convict possibly be, when he is

63

busted associating with a drug dealer selling smack on the street. Ralph lost his innocence a long time ago; all that's left of his future is a funeral. What a waste of a life! You have no idea how many times I wish he had walked away from drugs. I miss him.

"What we have done for ourselves alone dies with us;
what we have done for others and the world remains
and is immortal."

Albert Pike

Chapter Six

What I Should Have Learned From Uncle Rogelio

A drunk is a drunk is a drunk. Some are happy drunks, while others are often mean drunks. Some drunks get mellow when they drink, while others become loud. Some puke their guts out so often that their teeth start to corrode, while others just manage to hold everything down even though the world is spinning so violently that they can hardly walk. Some don't walk; they just get into their cars and drive while their world is a swirling blur. If they kill a pedestrian while in a drunken stupor, who cares? I often wonder if drunks worry about such things.

Do you wonder about those things too? Do any of your friends or relatives abuse alcohol? Have you learned anything from those you've seen have too much to drink? I wish I had paid a little bit more attention.

Uncle Rogelio was the Black Sheep of the family. The threat of being disowned by his mother was not his prime motivation for going north and joining the rest of the family in New York. The truth is that his life in Puerto Rico had been unfruitful and dangerous and he desperately needed the change.

My grandmother had all but given up hope in Uncle Rogelio. His drinking and gambling habits had made it very difficult for her to see any semblance of a prosperous future in Puerto Rico for Rogelio. Neither her parents nor her siblings were very forgiving or understanding of such vices or illnesses, especially when it came to Doña Hortensia's children. She was independent. She would have to deal with Rogelio's problems alone; bringing him to New York was best, she had hoped.

She was right, at least for a few years. Shortly after arriving in New York, Rogelio found a very good job. He started out as an apprentice in a mattress manufacturing plant and within a few years had been promoted to supervisor. He then met a young woman, got married, and used his savings to put a down payment on a house on Long Island. He also bought his first, brand new Oldsmobile. Rogelio was a diligent, hard working, and respected craftsman whose future looked very bright. Unfortunately, the brightness would all too soon begin to dim.

Judith, in my grandmother's opinion, didn't qualify to be a wife, certainly, not Rogelio's wife. In her eyes, Judith was crass, lacked respect for family elders, and was overtly manipulative to say the least. She refused to bear a child; a choice I'm sure my grandmother could not comprehend.

Judith was also a drunk whose drinking was often coupled with physical and verbal abuse of her husband. She would get drunk, insult his family, confront him, and invariably slap him around, usually in full view of family members and friends. Rogelio was not a coward. Regretfully, he loved his wife as much as he feared her. Mostly, he feared the thoughts of failure and of being alone.

Rogelio's life began a slow but definite downward spiral as he returned to his old vices. He began to drink, serious, whiskey-with-the-morning-coffee drinking. He maintained his foreman position for a while until his tardiness and eventual absence from work forced him out of a job.

Eventually, he ran out of money and prospects for a job. He sold his house and move to a blighted area of the Bronx. Occasional, menial jobs, welfare, and endless handouts from his mother kept him from being totally out on the streets. He frequently left Judith, only to return to her. When he did return he would be sober, clean, employed and enjoying a few dollars in his pocket. Unfortunately, he would allow the seesaw effects of his marriage, Judith's problems, and his own weaknesses to take charge of his life again.

I remember Rogelio least as a drunk and mostly as a loving uncle. I remember his many cars. My first driving experience was in one of Uncle Rogelio's cars. He packed a bunch of us kids in the car and gave each of us a turn at the wheel. The fact that we were on an old, country road without traffic didn't stop him from cautioning us on the rights and wrongs of driving. I was only seven years old and I still recall that short time behind the wheel. I was too short to reach the pedals and all I could do was steer while Uncle Rogelio pressed the brake and accelerator pedals. It was a great day in the country.

Uncle Rogelio had a passion for large, American cars. He was partial to General Motors' cars, especially Buick, Oldsmobile, and Pontiac. He had a new set of GM wheels every two to three years. I remember his 1959 Pontiac Catalina with trunk space equivalent to the size of a modern day import car. I especially remember his last, grand car, an Oldsmobile Delta 88. Uncle Rogelio would drive his "88" with the aplomb of a showman. He owned the road when he drove and if you got in his way he'd let you know about it, usually with a blast from the horn and a barrage of four-letter word insults. He feared no man on the road. When you're only five feet tall, driving a tank makes you feel invincible.

Several members of my family often called me "Negríto," meaning little black one. This is not an insult but an endearment common to boys (negríto) and girls (negríta) who are trigueño, meaning brunette and olive-skinned. Uncle Rogelio called me his "Dirty Nigger." That too was not an insult, not from him to me.

Whether sober or as drunk and as down as he ever became in my presence, Uncle Rogelio never failed to show me some measure of love, respect, and concern for my well being. When I asked for his bendición, a traditional old-world request for a blessing from one's elders, Uncle Rogelio never failed to acknowledge me.

My Uncle Rogelio was a happy, loud, rarely could walk a straight line, and always tried to drive – hard-core drunk. He drank from sunrise to sunset and then some, and yes, he drove while under the influence of alcohol. He was the king of road rage when he drove; but he never picked a fight. He may have been drunk most of the time; but he knew that at 5-feet, 115-pounds most of the world could kick his butt in a heartbeat.

To most people, Rogelio was someone to stay away from, someone to ridicule, and someone to point a finger at and say, "You don't want to grow up and be like him." Yet, he was my uncle and I loved him dearly.

Uncle Rogelio taught me a great deal about love and life. Unfortunately, I doubt that he knew that. He had a profound love for his family. He would hold a baby as gently as any mother on Earth could. If you were in pain, he would put his arms around you and take the suffering away and onto himself. Even in the middle of all that alcoholic fog, he would look at you and say the gentlest words of wisdom I've ever heard.

I should have paid better attention to the reception Uncle Rogelio received from everyone, family members and strangers alike, whenever he drank. Had I paid attention, instead of allowing my love for my uncle to cloud my perceptions, I would have learned some valuable lessons. The most important lessons I missed were that when drunks speak very few people listen. When drunks create a crafted piece of art from simple objects, most people will avert their eyes and miss enjoying a piece of beauty. Tragically, when drunks are sober, the dark cloud that hangs over them during their drunken episodes continue to deny them the rights they deserve as human beings; simple things like love, honesty, kindness, and forgiveness.

Had I paid attention to the total effects of my uncle's alcoholism, I would have never gone down the dangerous and near-fatal path that I did at the age of fifteen.

When I was fifteen years old, I'd boldly walk into any liquor store in the South Bronx, anywhere in Spanish Harlem and most places in Queens or Brooklyn and buy my fill of booze. Oh yeah, we were supposed to be carded, have our IDs checked; but we rarely were. A Puerto Rican kid like me, with a swanky mustache and a "so what" attitude, could just walk into most liquor stores or grocery stores and pick up a six-pack of beer without any questions. I think the storeowners thought we were tough kids they didn't want to mess with or they thought it was merely a right of passage – things us kids had to do as we grew up in the ghetto and prove we were men.

There's one piece of information about the accident I told you about in Chapter 2 that I've left out of the story. The night of the accident, as I stood in my living room ironing a shirt, Uncle Rogelio asked me what my plans were for the night. When I told him, he said he wouldn't permit me to go out that night. He explained that he had had a dream the previous night in which my brother Ralph was injured in an accident. I responded by giving him a lot of attitude and telling him that I could take care of myself Anyway, it was a dream about Ralph and that made it Ralph's problem.

My mother and uncle got into a nasty argument that night. She called his dream the delusions of a drunk, simple madness. He tore the shirt I had just finished ironing from my hands, arguing his position louder and louder; my mother laid into him with equal volume.

Uncle Rogelio was indeed sober that evening and I nearly died that night. My injuries were quite severe and recovery took several months. Uncle Rogelio never came to visit me during my convalescence, nor did he ever again confront his sister about her sons. I made a mistake. I'm sorry Uncle Rogelio. I should have listened to you.

Let me add up the cost of that one party. The recovery from my injuries took several months; consequently, I lost my entire junior year of high school. Prior to the accident, I dreamed of going to the Air Force Academy. Now with a scarred face, an injured back, a leg in a cast from my toes to my crotch, and a medical history of having been unconscious, the chances of being accepted into the Academy and then Undergraduate Pilot Training were gone. In an instant, I lost my most important dreams and I wasn't interested in setting any other goals.

I was sent away to my Uncle Salvador and Aunt Aida's house in Long Island, New York to recover from my injuries. For three months, they took care of me while I tried to figure out what course my life would take. Suddenly, I was fifteen years old and I didn't have a clue. I saw no goal worth pursuing.

Uncle Salvador drove me back to my mother's house in the Bronx just one week before I was supposed to visit my orthopedic surgeon and have my cast removed. It had taken every bit of those three months for my body to regain about 80% of its strength.

As soon as Uncle Salvador left my mother's apartment, I went to the bathroom, filled the bathtub with hot water, and then lowered myself into the tub, cast and all. I was tired of dragging that stinking cast around. I took a pair of scissors and cut the softened plaster and fabric as I removed the cast. I had places to go and people to see. Obviously, the dumb street-kid part of me hadn't learned much in those last three months.

I went out that evening to visit some friends, including the girl I was with at the time of the accident. I needed to know what was happening. I had to get back into the mix of things with my friends, and do some catching-up. Well guess what – the world had moved on without me.

"Hey, I'm back! You know me, the kid who almost died. I'm the person with all the scars on his face. Look at me, I still need crutches because my leg hurts and my knee won't bend when I try to walk. I took off my cast because I wanted to see you." My friends welcomed me back as if the accident hadn't happened. No pain and suffering, and my going away for three months hadn't happened. I went back home that evening confused.

It was March of 1965 and school was still in session. However, all I could do was sit at home wondering what I'd do until summer school started. I soon found my answer on the street – hang out with some of the high school and college dropouts in the neighborhood. Most of them spent their days promising their parents that they would return to school, while others promised to find a job and get off the street. What they all did every day was lie to their parents and friends. Their lying came easily as they took money from everyone and anyone to support their job-search expenses – drugs or alcohol.

Soon after I started hanging out with my new friends, I too created a story for anyone that asked me what my plans for my future were. I was going to find a good job while I waited for summer school to start. I found a great job flipping burgers and frying chicken at a take-out joint. I made just enough money to support my real job search – my next bottle of rum, scotch, wine, or beer. If it poured, I drank it!

Drinking rum didn't help define my passage from adolescence into adulthood. Drinking irresponsibly almost killed seven kids and I was one of the dummies in the car. Puking my guts out on a regular basis wasn't cool. I often embarrassed my straight friends, those that didn't drink nor use drugs. My drinking got so bad that my friends would take bets, whenever they invited me to their parties, as to how long it would take before their parents would ask me to leave. It wasn't long before my friends' parents didn't want me around their house or their kids.

O.K. so I lost sight of my original plans to go to the Air Force Academy. Was that a good reason to pull the plug on reality or to chip away at my self-respect? That's what I did every time I drank. I put off facing the reality that I didn't have a "Plan B" and that I had no choice but to set some new goals. All I did was delay reality with every drink I held in my hands – the reality that I needed to get off my butt and move on with my life.

Some of you may be wondering about a few things right about now. "Hey Mister, where were your parents while you were creating all this mess for yourself?"

Well my parents were divorced and I hadn't seen my father in several years. My mother and stepfather worked long hours and I was what some people called a "latch-key kid," at home on my own. Not that my mother didn't know I drank. I figured she just rationalized that it was better to have a son who drank than another son who was strung out on dope. Frankly, my mother and I never discussed my drinking. I knew that she would often slip into my room late at night, after I came home doing the drunken strut to my room, and she'd look for any evidence of drugs. I didn't do drugs so she accepted what she felt was the lesser evil – drinking.

Back then, I didn't consider the sense of resignation parents feel when they see their kids take a path that leads to nowhere. I was certainly on my way to nowhere as a fifteen and sixteen-year old. I spent the summer of '65 going to summer school early in the morning, Orchard Beach in the afternoon, and a part-time job at a candy store serving sodas and ice cream in the evening. Weekends were for parties, girls, and drinking. I would leave my house on Friday afternoons and return on Sunday afternoons.

Now there I was, in my mid-teens and staying out all weekend. Truthfully, I can't remember ever wondering if my mother was worrying about me. Hey, I had survived the car accident, I lost a year of school, and I was pissed-off at the world for screwing with my plans for the future. That's right! I was damn mad at what happened. All I wanted to worry about was myself. Why should I worry about anybody else? I had a younger brother; let him be my mother's hope for a proper family legacy. If all I had was one life to live, why not live it large?

I ignored the realities of where my conduct was leading me. I ignored any concept of self-discipline and quite obviously, I wasn't mature enough to accept the fact that I was responsible for me. That's right, me for me!

I wasn't holding myself responsible for my actions. I blinded myself to any vision into the future that would've helped me understand that every step I took defined my character, my future, and my legacy. I screwed up!

What were the steps that had led me down this path? I made a series of mistakes, took several wrong turns, crashed, burned, and foolishly disregarded the fact that every error pointed back at the decisions I had made. I can't excuse what I did; I knew exactly what I was doing.

I knew I shouldn't have been drinking at the party. My family often provided a small amount of alcohol to the kids at the dinner table. It was a way to share everything at the table as well as endorse the responsibility of knowing your personal and family boundaries.

Teenage drinking under the supervision and control of my elders was also permitted.

However, drinking outside of that family circle was frowned upon. You did so at the risk of embarrassment and a stern rebuke and isolation from the elders if you created a scene in public. Who cares about family elders and their advice? What do they know about being cool?

We'd buy a few six-packs of beer and then sit on the stoop of our apartment building and "slug" the beer down. My friends and I would often buy cheap booze and sneak it into a party or buy a few pints of rum, take our girlfriends to a movie, and drink while we made-out in the balcony section of the theater. We drank proudly, boldly and could care less about what people thought of us. In retrospect, what we really were was foolish and irresponsible.

When I was a teenage drunk, did my mother try to talk to me? Yeah, she did, but I didn't want to listen. In order not to hear her, I avoided her. I would lock myself in my room, claiming to be studying and doing homework. I'd disappear on weekends and try not to let her see me wasted, stumbling into the house late at night. I guess she didn't feel strong enough to stand in the doorway and say, "Enough is enough!" She had suffered so much with Ralph's drug habit and she still couldn't stop the flood of drugs from hitting him. My mother simply stood by me and hoped that time would fix things.

What measure of suffering did I bring into my mother's life? I had no right to do what I did. Nor did I have the right to lay waste to the hopes and expectations she had for me. No matter whether she stood at the door and said, "Enough!" I had no right!

I'm sure you sometimes find it hard to think and act from the same perspective as your parents. Seeing it their way isn't always easy. The truth is that there's a whole lot of distance between their then and your now. However, if you analyze their advice for its most basic element, you'll likely relate better to some if not all of that advice into your now. My grandmother used to tell me, "coger consejo," that if I listened to the counsel of the elders' I'd get to reach an old age. She never said I had to accept the counsel, just listen. I didn't listen well enough to my mom.

There were two people in my life that I thought had totally ignored my decline. I was falling and I was sure they had no idea of how far or how fast I was reaching bottom. Surprisingly, they did know and they were waiting for the right moment to let me know how they felt. The first one was my grandmother who with just a few words changed the course of my life.

Somehow, I had the presence of mind as I stood at the edge of a curb in the South Bronx holding on to the side of a car as best I could while I puked my brains out, to recognize that I had to find an exit to the miserable road I was already traveling down. I went home well past midnight and just crashed in my room; another wasted night. The next day, I found myself in my Grandma's kitchen.

That morning, as I sat at her kitchen table, Grandma said, "You are my grandson and I love you but I'm not proud of you. It's time for you to change and be the man I know you can be." She fried

77

some eggs for me and toasted some bread. Then, as she served me a cup of coffee, she said, "My greatest expectation of you is that you grow up and be a man I will respect."

I knew she loved me but it was in hearing and understanding her words, "…be a man I will respect," that stopped me in my tracks and forced me to think about what I was doing with my life.

The second person to bring a jolt of common sense to my life was a young girl, a redheaded teenager who I knew since I was five years old. She and I would date on occasion when she stayed at her older sister's place during summer vacation. Only two of my friends visited me in the hospital after the car accident; she was one of them.

Her name was Felicita Maldonado, a quiet, unassuming, shy girl from 102nd Street who let this street punk, me, into her life. It was during one of those summer visits, when a few of our friends teased her about dating "the guy who could drink anyone under the table." She didn't say anything to me right away. She knew I had lost a year of school and that my body had been racked up badly. She also knew of my dreams, of what I had hoped to be, and how those hopes seemed to disappear.

Later that day, in a private moment Felicita gently said, "I care for you very much, please stop drinking. Please stop hurting yourself." Then she held my hand and said, "Don't do this for me or for us, do it for you." No one else except for her and my grandmother had asked me to be a better me. I stopped drinking.

Please allow me to jump ahead a few years in my life's story and share something very special with you. In January 1978, I experienced what may have been one of my Uncle Rogelio's proudest moments of me and it's a memory that will last forever. Shortly after my having been commissioned a Second Lieutenant in the Air Force, I went back to New York City to visit my grandmother at her apartment. She had only seen me in uniform as a Staff Sergeant. That day, I wore the gold bars of a Second Lieutenant.

My Uncle Rogelio answered the door. He looked at me for the longest time without saying a word and then, he suddenly reached out and touched the gold bars pinned on my shoulders. Next, he gently ran his fingers across the medals on my chest. Finally, a smile came to his face and he gave me "Un fuerte abrazo," a strong embrace.

For most of the evening, Uncle Rogelio was very quiet, and yes, he was sober. He listened to me as I answered the questions from the family concerning my transition from being an Enlisted man to becoming an Officer and several questions about my future assignments. It wasn't until I was about to leave that he said something to me and he did so in front of the whole family. He said, "Don't ever forget where you came from. Don't ever forget that your family is proud of you. You have earned our respect and now you must earn the respect of those that work for you. Once you've done that, don't ever let anyone fail to render a proper salute to you. You are Boricua and an American military officer." With those words, Uncle Rogelio gave me his blessings; we embraced and said our good byes. There was no way for me to have known that those would be his last words to me.

The years passed quickly for Uncle Rogelio, taking their toll on him faster than most. His abuse of alcohol destroyed him. He died on March 10, 1980 at the age of 59. He had been hospitalized for a long time, suffering from cancer of the esophagus. He endured horrific pain during the terminal period of his illness as his body became frail and weak. My grandmother stood by his side over the endless weeks of hospitalization. I can't begin to know the pain she suffered watching her eldest son slip away. I can't begin to tell you what his death meant to me.

I had been on a remote Air Force assignment in Alaska during his rapid and all consuming illness. I had returned to Colorado, on a 30-day leave, and had taken my family to New Mexico for a brief vacation. He died while I was away on vacation; no one knew how to contact me. When I returned to Colorado, I called my mother to inquire about Uncle Rogelio. She told me his burial had been the previous day.

Years later, as I discussed Uncle Rogelio with my grandmother, she told me of her feelings of resentment toward me for not having been at her son's funeral. However, she understood the reasons for my not having been there. My grandmother also knew how he felt about me. How proud he was of me. How much it would have meant for him to see me one last time. My grandmother also knew that I had loved him and that just like her, I could always see beyond his weaknesses and find the goodness that lived within my uncle. She felt he needed more of us around him. I miss him dearly. Words can't express the loss I still feel today.

"Death devours all lovely things in fashion untimely."

Unknown

"What lies behind us and what lies ahead of us are tiny matters compared to what lives within us."

Oliver Wendell Holmes

Chapter Seven
Parents

If I were to ask you to tell me about your parents, it doesn't matter if they are adopted, foster, guardians, or your natural parents, and to describe to me what they were like as teenagers, could you do that? That's great if you can do it. If you can't give me a detailed account of them as kids, ask yourself why not. In either case, I'd like you to put this book down and go ask them to tell you a few stories about what is was like to be your age – thirteen, fifteen or whatever the case may be. Maybe you'll find out that they were "cool" kids – Oh Man, what a thought!

I didn't ask those kinds of questions when I was growing up. I wish I had. Maybe, then I would have had a better understanding of why my parents behaved the way they did. Maybe the memories of my childhood with them would be sweeter.

I wish I could say that all parents are perfect, but I can't. Mine surely weren't. Truthfully, I feel a bit of envy whenever I hear stories of how great someone's father or mother is. I didn't come from a broken home; it was more like a shattered home. Let me share with you a brief look into my parents' world and the influences they had on me during my childhood and well into my adulthood.

Carmen Lydia de la Rosa Rivera was my grandmother's third child and my mother. Today, as I look back on her life through somewhat mature and wiser eyes than those of a child, I can best describe her as a free spirit. I always saw that, even in my earliest recollections of my mother.

Free spirit can reflect a variety of behavioral traits, for Carmen its meaning was quite literal. She was a beautiful and intelligent woman who did whatever she wanted to do. Even as a young woman, she conducted herself well outside the norms of behavior relative to Puerto Rican society. Permissive and uncontrollable at an early age, she was married at the age of sixteen. Doña Hortensia recognized that her daughter's behavior was intolerable. Yet, Carmen would argue that her behavior was just an extension of what she had witnessed in her own mother, a struggle for independence.

Carmen married Raphael Alberto Cabrera, who fathered the first of her four children, Raphael Junior. Raphael Sr. was well aware of Carmen's amorous adventures prior to their marriage. Indeed, he had been one of her lovers. However, he had no insight into the level of independence Carmen would insist upon in their relationship. Unfortunately, Don Raphael had assumed that he would command a traditional role and rule his household. He made the classic macho assumption that his Latin wife would be a quiet homebody. That was a tragic mistake with this Latin woman.

Their marriage ended shortly after their arrival in New York. Carmen pressured Raphael beyond his capabilities, financially and socially. She had dreams of a house in the suburbs and a social life filled with the finer things in life. Carmen knew those finer things existed solely from reading magazines and seeing North American movies. Raphael was neither industrious nor motivated enough to pursue a course that would satisfy her needs. They were divorced within two years of marriage.

Carmen married her second husband, Miguel Angel Alicea in 1947. He's the father of Miguel Angel Jr., born in 1948 and José Manuel, yours truly, born in 1949. My mother's second marriage ended in divorce when I was 5-years old. My mother remarried two years later following the birth of her last son, Victor Velez de Rivera.

My mother's dream of the "American life" she had read about in magazines could never escape real-life realities during all her years of working alongside my grandmother at a lingerie factory in Manhattan's garment district. Those West Side factories were called "sweat shops;" earning their name by the cramped and unventilated environment, the pay-by-the-piece-sewn salaries, and the ever-vigilant shop stewards that monitored the progress of the day's quota while they coarsely kept these seamstresses at their machines.

When I was about seven or eight years old, I would often visit my grandmother and mother at work and be amazed by the speed of the women working at their sewing machines. They faithfully sewed their union's label on the waistbands of every finished piece of underwear. The sewing machines made a rhythmic noise and the women followed the beat as though it was choreographed.

The working conditions were the best concessions the labor unions could get, so they claimed, from the industry – women dressed in housecoats surviving non-air conditioned summers and unheated winters. There was very little change to those horrible scenes by the time Doña Hortensia retired in 1968.

I don't recall too much of my early childhood. However, as young as I may have been, I remember that one day my parents were living under the same roof; the next day they weren't. I've never heard of any kid having a vote as to whether their parents get divorced. Michael and I surely didn't.

The last time I saw my Dad, I was twelve years old. What have I missed in the last fifty-one years since then? It's not so much what I've missed, rather what my father has missed. He missed my swimming on the high school team and lettering in sports. He missed my wedding and the birth of my three daughters. He missed my graduation from college when I received my Bachelor of Science Degree in Aerospace Science and the ceremony when I received my Master of Science Degree in Business.

My father missed the swearing-in ceremony when I enlisted in the Air Force and the pinning-on of my Second Lieutenant rank when I was commissioned as an officer. I was the first in my family's history to receive such an honor and he wasn't around to share that moment with me. Had he been around fifteen years after my commissioning, he would have been with me when I received the news that I had been selected for promotion to the rank of Lieutenant Colonel.

My father never saw me in uniform, he never saw the medals on my chest, and he never had the opportunity to say, "That's my boy!" He wasn't at my family's side when I was shipped overseas during the war. Nor was he waiting for me upon my return.

Another special moment in my life that my father missed was the ceremony honoring my retirement from the Air Force; a ceremony with 150 guests from across the United States. Most importantly, he missed the presentation of two shadow boxes. The first box was a display case containing all the medals, ranks, and insignias I had earned while in uniform. The second shadow box contained a flag that had been flown in my honor over the Capitol of the United States in Washington, DC – our Nation's flag. My father missed all that.

How do I know he missed all those important moments? It was in those moments that I missed my father the most. That's how! Deep inside my mind, I had reconciled the fact that he wasn't ever going to be around. I would have to be satisfied with the presence of those people whom I felt were important to share those special moments with – my wife and children, family, my friends and associates.

My father wasn't the only parent absent from each of my celebrations; with the exception of my wedding, my mother was absent as well. My mother missed them because of her sense of priorities. Those events were all successes, my successes. However, she had three other sons to help steer their course, if not toward success, at least toward survival.

I know my mother didn't ignore my successes. Whenever I visit my mother, her friends always tell me how she brags about my achievements. Nevertheless, bragging about and sharing the moments aren't and will never be the same. What I've always done is draw a tighter circle around those I feel are important to me and then take as much joy as I can in sharing my life's moments with them.

Over the years, my children have developed a very negative attitude toward their paternal grandmother. Who is she really? They'll never know. Whenever my children questioned my mother's sense of priorities, I answered, "She's done the best she knows how." I believe that. I love my mother, unquestionably, even though she's never been the ideal mom depicted on TV, in novels, or magazines.

Obviously, parents make mistakes too. I want you to ask yourself, whom do you hold responsible for your successes? I think you have to hold yourself responsible and no one else. Each of us has to wake up every day, swing our feet over the side of the bed, and greet the new day along with all the goodness as well as every bit of crap it may bring into our lives.

When you were a baby, your parents wrapped you in blankets, like a cocoon, in order to help you feel safe, secure, and warm. As a toddler, they watched over your every step, making sure, you didn't play with matches, the electrical sockets, or the cleaning fluids so many people keep under the kitchen sink. Your safety was their number one concern.

Now, as a teenager, they've turned you loose, at least it seems that way, so that you can go off on your own and get an understanding of independence – a chance to grow up. From whom do you learn independence or some sense of growing up? Should it be your peers, teenagers who are still learning about independence, who should serve as your mentors?

Let's assume that you're feeling a sense of having been turned loose as I was at the age of twelve. It's not that your parents don't care about you; they haven't abandoned you. They just think you need some room to grow. Sadly, many parents make this mistake. You might need to help them help you. Tell your parents that this is not the time for you to be free falling through life. Pull the ripcord and get that canopy, that gentle umbrella, your parents, back into your life. Tell them you appreciate the space and freedom they've given you; but you need their wisdom and insight. You need them as a parachute to help you land safely into adulthood. Whatever you do, don't become arrogant and bitter, and say, "Hey, I've done O.K. so far without them. Who needs them? I'll be out of here soon enough!"

I screwed up because I wasn't persistent or insistent. I didn't apply any pressure to my parents. I didn't challenge them with requests for more of their time, a little bit of focus on their son's need for some adult leadership. I shut the doors to parental support with my smart-ass attitude; yet I expected them to reach out and keep me from falling on that smart ass. Obviously, I share a good chunk of the blame.

Challenge yourself by bringing your parents back into your circle. Help them help you. By bringing your parents closer to you, you may be able to see a little bit of the world through their eyes. Your parents might be able to see through your eyes too if you open up and give them some insight into what's happening in your world. Wow, think of the possibilities! You can help your parents be better parents as they try to help you be a better you.

In all fairness to good parents, those that try to provide guidance and who reach out to their children when they see them headed in the wrong direction, I need to say, thank you.

Whether my parents were perfect or not, that wasn't good enough a reason for me not listening to them. The best that they could do was to provide me some insight into what life is all about. I forgot that they were kids once too. I'm sure my parents often recalled the mistakes they made as teenagers and the pain that those mistakes brought to their families and themselves. I have to believe that my mother did her best to keep me from going through that pain too. I just wish they had shared those recollections with my brother and me. Maybe, we could have learned from their mistakes without having to make so many mistakes of our own. Fortunately, my struggles through the self-inflicted troubles of my youth taught me a great deal about parenting, especially about how I would conduct myself with my children.

Soon after Michael and I graduated from the eighth grade and were on our way to freshman year in high school our family broke up. Victor's dad and our mother had divorced a few years earlier and suddenly my mother decided to remarry again. That's right, husband number four, and stepfather number two and still I didn't have a vote! There was just one major problem with her decision; the rest of the family didn't have a vote either and they rejected her choice for a husband.

As I can best remember and describe it to you, the dislike for my mother's husband was instant and total. My grandmother, being the direct and independent woman she was, packed up all her belongings and took my aunt Maria Dolores, my cousin Aida Luz, my brothers Michael and Victor with her to an apartment in the Bronx. One day we were a family, the next day we were distant relatives.

My immediate family went from eight to three overnight yet somehow, that didn't bother me. I remember thinking the whole mess was grownup stuff and that it would all blow over quickly. It didn't. My world had changed. It was a change I had no control over. I wasn't asked for an opinion and if I had one, I wasn't sure it would've made any difference. I didn't get a vote!

I do remember Grandma asking me if I wanted to go with her and the rest of the family. As I think about it today, that wasn't a fair question to ask a thirteen-year old kid. Moreover, even though my aunt, Maria Dolores, was the one that truly raised me, somehow I felt my place was with my mother.

My mother and stepfather, Eddie, enjoyed their lives. They went to restaurants and movies, to the racetrack, and boxing matches while I stayed at home. Considering my options of going and arguing with Eddie (I never called him Dad) or staying at our apartment, watching TV, reading or studying, staying at home was a better choice. I often resented the long days and evenings I spent alone in that apartment on 98th Street.

I can clearly recall the many nights that I sat on the platform of the fire escape watching the traffic along Lexington Avenue. Fire escapes are snake-like, steel ladders found on the front or back of old buildings and were designed for use as emergency exits. I could see for miles from the fifth floor platform. I'd watch the bright headlights of cars coming toward me and then I'd watch the glow of their red taillights as they drove past me. That sense of people coming and going intrigued me. I often wondered if my days of going would come soon.

Eventually, my frustrations grew too much for me to deal with. One incident brought it all to a head; my stepfather got mad at me and slapped me across the face. I just stared at him coldly and said to him, "If you ever touch me again, I swear, I'll stab you in the heart." I was a thirteen-year old street kid and very capable of such violence.

My mother responded by grabbing my arm and spinning me around. Before she could say a word, I said, "Mom, he may be your husband, but he'll never be my father!" The confrontation ended there; Eddie and I never spoke to each other again.

As I look back upon that day, it wasn't that my stepfather was a bad man or that I was just a quick-mouth kid with an attitude. It was really a matter of his inability to communicate at my age level and my refusing to listen to what he was really trying to say. Two wrongs never make a right! It was soon after that battle, that my stepfather moved us to an apartment in the South Bronx.

Our apartment was on the first floor of a four-story tenement building; a great place to sit on the windowsill and watch the world go by. My neighborhood consisted of interracially mixed, low-income families living in old apartment buildings or high-rise projects, the street name for subsidized public housing. There wasn't much difference between the Bronx and Manhattan, not when you compared El Barrio to the South Bronx – a war zone is a war zone!

The one, truly good thing about moving to the Bronx was that I was closer to my grandmother and the rest of the family. I missed hanging out with Michael. He had enrolled at Cardinal Hayes High School in the Bronx and I had enrolled at Aviation High School in Queens. We were now separated at home and at school and those were realities I had trouble accepting. However, all I could do was to take as many opportunities as I could to go see my grandmother and hang out with Michael. The subway ride was only $.50 cents roundtrip.

My grandmother lived on Longfellow Avenue and 174th Street. She had moved the family into a predominantly Jewish neighborhood and that made for exciting visits. Please understand that up to this point in my life I had been raised in a predominantly

Hispanic, Roman Catholic environment. Except for what I had learned from the nuns in school, I had no idea what Judaism was about. Another treat, and for a 13-year old city kid whose hormones were raging it was a big treat – the girls that Michael introduced me to were different from the girls in the South Bronx. Different girls from a different culture and religious background; I had a lot to learn. I looked forward to every visit to Grandma's place.

That's how it went throughout my high school years; I'd ride the subway to 174th Street and Southern Boulevard, walk a few blocks to my grandmother's house, and visit the rest of the family. Sadly, I don't remember Grandma or Michael visiting my house in the South Bronx more than a handful of times in all the years we lived there.

In the name of fair play between parents and their children, let me take a small step backwards and speak to you about the tragedy of at least one child trying to live up to his family's expectations. The piece of my family's history that I'm about to share with you is about conflict between old and young; the traditions of the elders and the desires of the young to break from those traditions.

You may see some resemblance in this story to things that have happened in your family. I ask that you keep one thing in your mind as you read this section – both sides were right and both sides were wrong. I think you'll be able to figure the rest out by yourself.

There has been a long-standing tradition in my family that the eldest son, at a time chosen by the family's elders, is bestowed the honor of becoming the chief negotiator and arbitrator, counselor and spokesperson of the family. It's like the passing of the baton in a medley relay. Once the elders had reached a point in their lives at which they were ready to relinquish the day-to-day affairs of the family to someone younger, they would put their chosen candidate through a series of tests. If the candidate succeeded, the baton was passed.

He or she, who holds the baton in a race, holds the success or failure of the team in their hand. Likewise, he or she who speaks for the family has a tremendous amount of influence on the family and plays a critical part in its future. In some form or other, such a passing of this influential role is found in just about every culture I've ever encountered.

One is not expected to reject the tests that come with such traditions. Nor is one expected to decline the offer to sit at the head of the table. To reject such a position within the family is considered an insult, an insult not easily forgotten or forgiven by the elders. The candidate is expected to accept the assignment enthusiastically.

Michael rejected it all. He was the second oldest son. Ralph, the oldest son, had already failed in life; his drug use had sealed his fate. There would be no offer made to him. Therefore, it became Michael's turn. His task was to legitimize the family's traditions and step up to the tests and succeed. That challenge came at a time in Michael's life that was filled with many other challenges. He couldn't and wouldn't accept any more. Predictably, his rejection set him at odds with the family elders.

The elders' needs for adherence to tradition drove Michael away from the family. In a few short years, he found himself needing to leave the family far behind. I saw all this happen. When Michael left the family, he left me too. It took sixteen years before I was reunited with my brother.

I understood what Michael went through then and I understand what some kids are going through now as they sense a confrontation between family tradition and the ways of today. I often think back and try to examine what affects family traditions may have had on Ralph. I won't blame his drug abuse on the family; drugs were his choice and his alone. Nevertheless, what about his music; did he play well because he had a passion inspired from within or did he play to please the family? Was his youth taken away with the endless hours of lessons and practice? To be fair, I think only Ralph can answer those questions.

My grandmother had all but given up on selecting an heir to the lead position within the family. I wasn't aware of my being evaluated by my elders nor did I anticipate the family approaching me for that position, but they did. I was older then, married with children and serving in the U.S Air Force. My grandmother called me to her house and spoke to me about my duty to my family. She said, "The foolishness and stupidity of your youth are gone. You have grown to be a responsible man, exactly what you needed to be in order to do what the family will ask of you." Yes, they tested me, and no, I never failed them. I assume whatever duties they give me and fulfill them as an honor.

"There is a destiny that makes us brothers. No one goes his own way; all that we send into the lives of others, comes back into our own. The crest and crowning of all good, Life's final star is Brotherhood.

Edwin Markham

Chapter Eight
Brotherhood

I didn't hang out much with the kids from my South Bronx neighborhood. I stayed to myself during much of the school year. When I wasn't studying at home, I was out visiting a girlfriend or hanging out with Michael, Felix, or Jimmy.

Michael and I shared our brotherhood with a couple of our classmates. Felix Salgado, Jr. and Jose Jimenez, Jr. were more than just two boys from the "block." Michael and I stayed "tight" with them throughout our school years and the decades beyond. Even today, our individual families are united; not by blood but by the same ties that brought our families together in El Barrio.

Felix lived within walking distance of my apartment and Jimmy lived near Michael's apartment. Together, the four of us formed a solid Brotherhood. We helped each other with our homework, we introduced each other to new girls, we'd laugh at each other's teenage screw-ups, and sometimes we argued amongst ourselves. The arguments never lasted very long. We saved our energy for anyone or anything that tried to beat the Brotherhood down. Man, if you messed with one of us, you messed with the four of us! Maybe we had seen too many movies about the Three Musketeers, one for all and all for one. Nonetheless, an unwritten rule and an unspoken alliance existed – you didn't mess with any of us!

Here's an example of one of the many times we watched each other's back as kids on the streets. Soon after Michael moved to Longfellow Avenue, he started dating a young Jewish girl named Debbie. My grandmother didn't really like the idea that anyone in her traditional Roman Catholic family would consider dating someone outside of our culture or religion. I dated a Jewish girl too and whenever Michael and I went to a synagogue with our girlfriends, our grandmother would insist we go to church and confess having been in a Jewish temple. Grandma wouldn't accept our argument that it was the same God, regardless of the house of worship. Michael and I never confessed our visits to Jewish synagogues, AME Baptist Gospel, or Protestant Pentecostal services. We went to religious services with all our girlfriends. The girls and their parents ate that stuff up!

Michael and Debbie had a good thing going until her folks decided to move to another neighborhood. Pelham Parkway is the name of a main thoroughfare that cuts through a part of the Upper Bronx. The neighborhoods surrounding the parkway were distinctively Jewish, back in the 1960s.

Michael would make frequent trips to Pelham Parkway to visit Debbie. Unlike my dark hair and olive skin, Michael has blond hair and his skin tone is very fair, similar to our father. Michael never had trouble entering neighborhoods such as Pelham Parkway. Surprisingly, a group of young punks got in Michael's face during one of his trips to see Debbie. After a lot of name-calling and threats about having his butt kicked should he ever return to Pelham Parkway, the punks told Michael that he had better bring an army on his next trip. That was a mistake.

That night Michael called me, I called Felix, and Felix called Jimmy. The next Saturday night, forty Puerto Ricans, Cubans, Dominicans, African Americans, and a few of our Jewish friends from Longfellow Avenue descended on Pelham Parkway. We broke up into three groups; think about it, street kids with war plans. Some of us rode our bikes, some took the subway, and others arrived by bus. Somehow, we managed to arrive within a few minutes of each other. Michael did get to see Debbie briefly that night.

The punks who had confronted Michael a few days earlier had seen the army-of-forty, ran home to their parents, and immediately called the police. Getting to Pelham Parkway was easy that night. Leaving was a bit busy considering the red, white, and blue flashing lights of the dozen or so police cars responding to a few unfriendly visitors in a usually peaceful neighborhood.

Michael never had any trouble visiting Debbie again.

You would think that as much as we protected each other we'd never play pranks on one another. Guess again.

Jimmy and I went to Aviation High School in Queens together. Jimmy being the quiet, reserved kid that he was, rarely got in any trouble with the teachers or other students. Jimmy had one of those youthful, innocent faces that made you think he was too young and too smart to get into any trouble. I, on the other hand, being somewhat of a clown in school, would never be mistaken for being innocent. I was always in some sort of mix with the teachers.

My smart mouth got me in more trouble than it was worth. It didn't matter if we were in school, riding the subway, at parties, or at the beach; I'd raise some crap with a stranger and get Jimmy involved too, just to see how he'd react. Jimmy was always cool about the whole thing and we'd laugh for days about how I managed to get him involved in one of my practical jokes. I'm glad Jimmy had a great sense of humor and tolerated all of my clowning around.

There are two stories involving Jimmy that I've told many times, especially whenever the Brotherhood got together. As old as the stories are, telling them somehow brought us back together every time and we gladly relived some of those crazy days as teenagers.

The first story took place on a subway in the Bronx. The 149th Street and 3rd Avenue station used to be a major connection for two subway lines and two bus lines. The area around the station was a shopping district where many of the people from the South Bronx bought clothes, furniture, shoes, and food. There was always quite a bit of subway passenger and pedestrian traffic too. All these factors made it a crowded and busy thoroughfare for people, cars, busses, and trains.

Jimmy and I were returning home to the Bronx after having spent a Saturday morning in Spanish Harlem. When our train pulled into the 149th Street station, a large number of passengers got off the train and an even larger number of passengers got on. Jimmy and I had been standing in the center of the train as the passengers got off and on the train. As the doors closed and the train started to move, one of the new passengers, a Hispanic woman who happened to be standing next to Jimmy noticed that her purse was open. As she searched the contents of her bag, she noticed that her wallet was missing. That's when the not so smart, smart-ass clown seized an excellent opportunity to get Jimmy in trouble.

Speaking in Spanish, the woman anxiously asked everyone near her to look around the floor of the train for her missing wallet. Without skipping a beat, I looked Jimmy straight in the eye and said, aloud in English, "Jimmy, give it back." The look on his face was priceless. In an instant, we had drawn the attention of the other passengers.

Suddenly, the other passengers were staring at Jimmy. They spoke to each other in Spanish, openly questioning if this young kid could have taken the woman's wallet. Jimmy and I heard the Spanish words that were being said. Once again, I looked at Jimmy and again said, "Jimmy, give it back."

This time Jimmy looked back at me and the look wasn't calm but a bit frightened. He then said, "Bro, stop messing around. I don't have the wallet."

I believe I'm much wiser today than I was that day on the subway and I surely wouldn't play that trick on anyone but what I did next to Jimmy was as close to evil as one can get. When Jimmy asked me to stop all I could do was answer back with a stern look, "Jimmy, give it back." Now, several passengers were openly accusing Jimmy, in Spanish, of being a thief. We were fortunate that our train was pulling up to another subway station. I grabbed Jimmy by the arm and we got off the train. Needless to say, Jimmy was pissed off, big time, at me. Moreover, when word got back to our neighborhood about what I did, everybody teased Jimmy for letting me get away with it. Thank God, Jimmy had a sense of humor.

You might assume that this second story would've lost its ability to draw a laugh after all these years. It hasn't. Strangers would consider the gag I pulled on Jimmy as nasty, crude, and rude. Maybe so; but Jimmy was my brother. He knew that I would never hurt him or let anyone else hurt him. Jimmy always laughed whenever I told this story.

In the 1960's, Section One of Orchard Beach in the Bronx was a Latino haven. English was not spoken in that section, Spanglish maybe, but definitely no English. All the kids would come up from Spanish Harlem and the South Bronx to groove on Latin Jazz played live by a variety of Puerto Rican and Cuban musicians. Caribbean food and some ice-cold Cuba Librés were always available.

When Jimmy was a teenager, he fell in love as often as the rest of the guys. However, unlike most of the guys, when Jimmy fell in love it was head-over-heels, big time love. Each new girlfriend was the girl of his dreams. He was with one of the girls of his dreams when we took a trip to Orchard Beach.

There had to be about fifteen of us from Longfellow and Bryant Avenues who went to the beach that day. Jimmy was dating a new girl, a petite, blond kid from Manhattan who was the cousin of Lila and Bonnie, two good friends of ours. The day's activities had been typical; we danced on the sand, fooled around in the water, played beach games, and just hung out in Section One. If a couple wanted to make out in private, they usually went out in the water where they were left alone to do their thing. It really wasn't considered cool to be making out on a blanket in full view of everyone. Jimmy's date apparently didn't like to swim, so they slipped under a large beach blanket as their answer to privacy. Yes indeed, I seized another opportunity.

I noticed that the two silhouettes under the blanket had become one tangled bundle of legs, arms, and torsos. Jimmy and his girlfriend were well into a serious make-out session. That's when I quietly asked the rest of the guys and gals to surround the blanket covering the tangled pair. I then grabbed a corner of the blanket and yanked it off the couple. Before Jimmy could say a word, I yelled at him, "Jimmy, you should be ashamed of yourself, taking advantage of this young girl." Then I said, "Young lady, are you sure that this young man has honorable intentions? You don't know him as well as we do."

Then I turned my attention back to Jimmy, who by this time was lying on his back laughing and saying to everyone, "Why me?"

I then said, "Jimmy, shame on you!" I finished it all by jumping on the blanket and giving Jimmy a kiss. Jimmy was laughing as hysterically as was the rest of the gang. The girlfriend, red-faced and mad, just had a few choice words for me, words that aren't fit to print.

The Brotherhood studied hard at school and we played hard at home. Felix and Michael were two serious party animals. Jimmy and I always credited them for teaching us some fine dance moves. Felix, like Michael, loved to dance. It was on the dance floor where Felix and Michael conquered the girls.

Even to this day, Felix who is now in his fifties still jumps up and does the Mash Potato and the Twist. Moreover, he can still do a mean Merenque, a shake-your-booty dance that originated in the Dominican Republic. I won't tell you any love stories concerning Felix. I've been sworn to Brotherhood secrecy never to give a hint of Felix ever having had more than one girlfriend at the same time.

Within the Brotherhood, I'm certain only one of us ever followed the one-girl-at-a-time rule and he was the same guy that always fell head-over-heels in love. I will not claim fidelity in the conduct of the other guys. We were all bad boys. We may not have dated more than one girl in the same borough but New York City had five boroughs.

Felix's mom and dad, just as Jimmy's parents were surrogate moms and dads to Michael and me. It was Don Felix, Felix's dad, who counseled us about drinking, admonishing us to keep our heads on our shoulders and guard ourselves against any foolishness that we couldn't recover from. Doña Carmen Lydia, Felix's mom, fed us some of the best Puerto Rican food on the planet. Her gentle and caring ways brought out the "gentle-man" in us as a sign of respect.

Felix was our soldier; a sense of humor coupled with a kick-ass attitude that he could easily back up. You messed with Felix only once, only fools tried it twice. If he said, "I've got your back," your back was covered. Whenever we went to a movie, a dance, the beach, or just hung around the block, Felix was on guard.

We were in our mid-teens when Felix and I went shopping in the North Bronx and I got into an argument with a salesperson. For some unknown reason, the salesperson didn't want to accept my down payment on a jacket that I planned to pick up after the alterations were completed. I would then pay the remainder of the bill, assuming the alterations were correct. The salesperson kept insisting on full payment in advance. I asked to see the manager and when he arrived, I continued questioning the practice of refusing to accept a down payment.

All the while, Felix had observed another salesperson staring at me. Felix walked up to the man and said, "I've seen you staring at my friend. What's your problem? Do you like him? Do you want to kiss him?" Felix got right in the man's face and then asked, "Don't you like me? Don't you want to kiss me too?" I know Felix sensed the salesperson was sizing me up and Felix just wanted to provoke him. I knew it had become time to get the hell out of there. You just didn't mess with Felix's brothers.

Felix always had a logical argument for every confrontation. I remember one subway ride back to the Bronx following a day visiting some friends in El Barrio. Michael, Jimmy, Felix and I boarded the train at 110th Street for the two-stop trip to 125th Street where we had to switch trains for one headed to the Bronx. As we waited on the platform, a man, who had the look of a cop, approached us and asked, "What station did you boys catch the train at?"

Before any of us could answer, Felix asked the man, "Are you a cop?" That's when the fun started.

Without showing us any identification, the man continued with another question, "Did you guys pay a fare, or did you jump the turnstiles for a free ride?"

Again, Felix interrupted before we could answer and asked, "Are you a cop?"

Meanwhile, the rest of us were trying not to crack up; we just went along for the ride. The man really seemed agitated at this point and as he was about to ask yet another question, Felix jumped in and again asked, "Are you a cop?"

The poor man lost it. He gave Felix a nasty look and replied, "No! I'm a sanitation worker."

That's when Felix finished him off by saying, "Well if you're not a cop, why are you asking us any questions?" Logic won and the man turned red and just walked off. I didn't learn to be a smart-ass from Felix, but man, I love his style.

The Brotherhood split up for a few years following high school, not by intent but by necessity. Felix joined the Marine Corps and left for boot camp shortly after graduation. Two months later, Jimmy joined the Corps too and left for boot camp. Michael, who was exempt from the military draft due to asthma, had a falling-out with the family and left for Pennsylvania. I was the first to get married and after a few years, I joined the Air Force. Miles may have separated us for a while but we put it all back together on the day that Michael got married many years later. Hearing the other wedding guest refer to us as brothers made us look at each other and say, "Yeah, that's right! Once you have it, it never goes away."

When Michael left for Pennsylvania, I lost a very close relationship with my brother that I had grown up depending upon. After fifteen years of separation, Jimmy found Michael in Philadelphia. Jimmy was the one who helped Michael see a better view of his life's picture. By this time, Felix, Jimmy and I had been married and each of us had children. Michael had missed all that.

About one year after Jimmy found Michael, my daughter, Elloise, enlisted in the U.S. Navy. She visited her Uncle Jimmy in New Jersey right after completing training and just prior to her being shipped overseas to Rota, Spain. Jimmy took Elloise to meet her

Uncle Michael. Six months later, Michael flew to Germany, where I was stationed, and met his other two nieces. The reunion wasn't difficult; we've recovered those lost years and my daughters have come to know and love their Uncle Michael.

I can only offer one possible course of remedy to you about the issues of family traditions and expectations. Talk it out. Let your family know how you feel. Tell them of your aspiration, your hopes for the future, and your needs for today. They may not accept or understand your goals and your needs may conflict with their traditional ways, but at least you've given them a view of the path you've chosen to take. I hope that they will give you their blessings. That's better than turning your back on your family, much better than leaving your brothers behind.

Brothers and sisters are like best friends that just happen to live with you. If you're lucky, those best friends that aren't related to you will often fill your life just like brothers and sisters do too. Treasure them all.

Lady Liberty, the face that greeted thousands of families to the United
States of American; my family was one of them

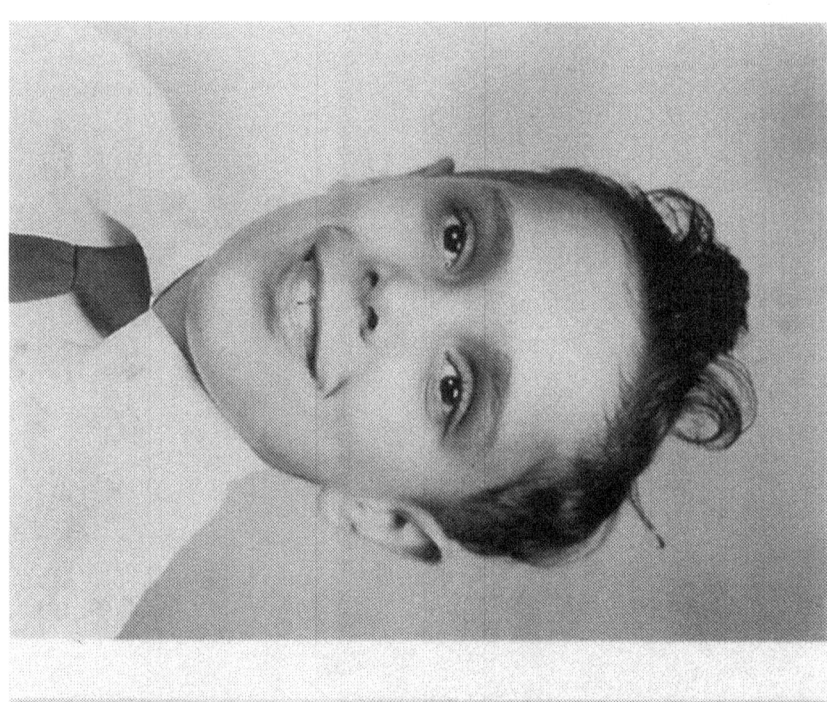

Michael and Joseph Alicea, the Salt and Pepper Twins

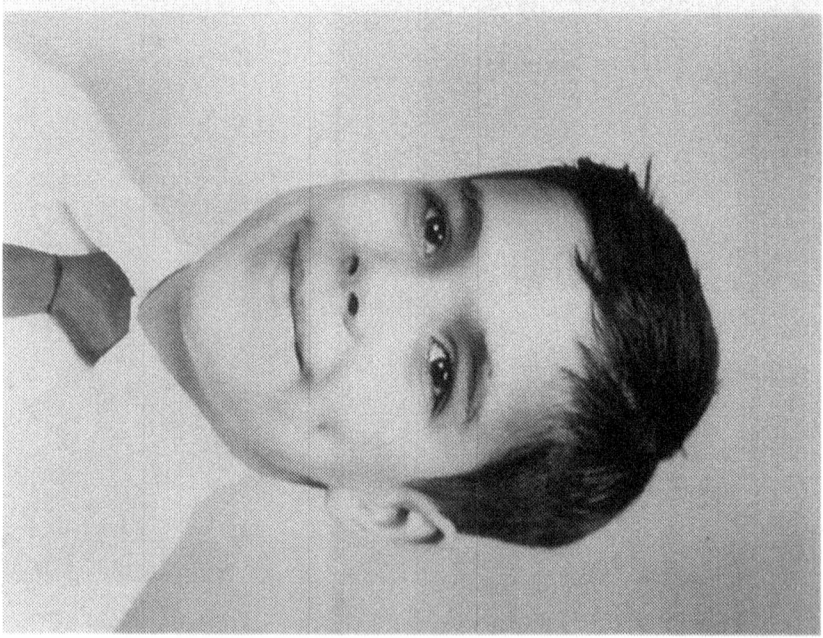

Airman Salvador Alonso and Doña Hortensia de la Rosa

My oldest brother, Raphael Cabrera; once a young and gifted artist

Uncles Salvador and Rogelio; my surrogate fathers

Felicita Maldonado, that young red-haired girl that changed my life

My last look at New York before I joined the U.S. Air Force, the
Twin Towers and the Empire State Building in the background –
The Spirit of America lives on

From Airman to Officers, I retired as a major and my dear friend Jerry Browning (far right) retired as a lieutenant colonel

The last meeting of the Brotherhood- Felix Salgado, Michael Alicea, Joseph Alicea, and José "Jimmy" Jimenez

A child walks the same streets I did—may his steps be well chosen, purposeful, and blessed

"A relationship is like a rose,

How long it lasts, no one knows;

Love can erase an awful past,

Love can be yours, you'll see at last;

To feel that love, it makes you sigh,

To have it leave, you'd rather die;

You hope you've found that special rose,

'Cause you love and care for the one you chose."

Rob Cella

Chapter Nine
Lovers or Apprentice Mechanics

How wonderful it is being young, in love, and dreaming of living happily ever after. The sight of a teenage couple holding hands brings a smile to older folks as they recall their days of young love. Behind those smiles, many of those folks may be reliving memories from their younger days when they yearned for the love of someone special. Has that feeling of love or yearning happened to you too?

As a teenager, I fell in love dozens of times, actually, more like thousands of times. I don't doubt that you have or will too. Most teenagers are a bit unsuspecting about Mother Nature; the way she plays that L-O-V-E game with everyone. She surely played my strings well. All the guys on my block knew that our bodies were changing, our hormones started raging, and we suddenly found time to notice girls and realize that they weren't the enemy. The girls in the neighborhood, who'd matured early, physically, and probably a bit mentally too when compared with boys, all of a sudden invited us boys into their inner circles. We were no longer the enemy. Then LOVE bloomed! At least that's what we were led to believe.

All the greeting card companies spoke, in those days as they do today, of "Young Love" – they even manufactured Valentine's Day cards for kindergarten children. I still remember the way cartoons and TV shows bombarded us with love themes back when I was in elementary school. Toy manufactures sold thousands of dolls, many of which were anatomically correct, selling the idea of boy meets girl. Then the toy makers flooded the market with infant-like animated dolls that ate, drank, and actually dirtied their diapers too; creating an impression, that parenting was easy.

I wonder if the toy industry really meant for us kids to think, "Hey, I can take care of this doll. I guess that means I can take care of a real baby, right?"

By the time I reached high school, I became a believer of all the make-believe "they lived happily forever after" found in books, cartoons, comic strips, movies, and TV show advertising. I was a teenager in love! I fell in love with classmates, friends of classmates, their sisters, their sister's friends, and every other girl I saw, met, and looked at from across the aisle in a bus, a train or at church. I even fell in love with girls I had only heard about. All that may sound weird, but LOVE was in bloom. My body was ready; I had muscles, a mustache, and a few whiskers on my chin, hair in my armpits and my voice had changed. I was ready for love!

Wrong Oh, Buck-Oh! The truth is that I, along with most other teenagers, was too naïve to accept that the human body's transition from childhood through adolescence and into maturity was a long process. At best, all my friends and I were qualified for when we reached the frontier of adolescence was Apprentice Mechanic. Mother Nature gave our bodies and a very small chunk of our brains' gray matter some basic instructions on the mechanics of sex – part "A" goes with Part "B." Ironically, that part of our brains that is coded with evolution's signatures and behavioral data only helps us perform the physical act, which is what sex is.

Did I really know what I was doing? Most importantly, did I know what I didn't know? Was I missing something? What could possibly be missing? Boy meets girl, both are willing, and the deed was done. Wasn't that all that was necessary?

The most important thing I, as a kid passing through puberty, didn't know, understand, believe in, or remind myself of every time I considered having a physical relationship with someone was that there would always be more to love than simple mechanics. Some of the words I heard often, while I shined all those shoes in bars, were that love is compassion, empathy, commitment, truth and so much more. The last thing I needed to deal with was more of that adult stuff. Stuff I was still struggling to understand.

Sexually active fourteen year-old kids from the South Bronx in the 60's were not rare. At least I didn't consider myself as being rare. We, teenagers, spent too much time making sure we dressed well, smelled good, acted cool, and knew how to party. Parties were our special way of spending time with each other, having fun and maybe meeting new kids. We were bold though. Boys made it obvious; having sex was the goal. Girls acted shyly; but they knew what the boys were after. Moreover, while the girls may have seemed demure and gentile, they'd kick your butt if you stepped out of line. Getting to first base wasn't difficult; beyond that, getting to other bases required finesse and a very willing partner. Nothing else was cool.

Our parties were special. No matter where we held the party, the bright, white light bulbs were changed to dark reds and blues. The music was always a mix of slow-dancing hits from the 50's and early 60's, Little Anthony and the Imperials, the Platters, Don and Juan, and Smoky Robinson and the Miracles. The Five Satins' hit from the 50's, "In the Still of the Night," was my all-time favorite. Imagine the lies you could tell a girl as you held her close while dancing slowly listening to the Five Satins sing, "In the still of the night, I held you, held you tight. Cause I love, love you so." You wouldn't believe the heat two teenage bodies could generate after an hour of that s-l-o-w music. Hot enough to cook!

As a kid, I went to a good number of school dances and parties at friends' apartments in the city. I'd take a date or meet some girls there and after a couple of hours of soft and slow music, plus loads of street-jive garbage, better known as lies, I did my best to conquer the virtue of my dance partner. Hey, it was the thing any hot-blooded, hormone raging, got-to-sow-my-oats teenaged boy, had to do at that point in his life. I know there was no truth in anything I said during those slow dances.

I met a young girl that was new to the neighborhood at one of those parties. She was a cute, blond, junior high school kid. We danced, I gave her the usual street-kid, bold face lies, and soon we were making out right on the dance floor. We spent the next few weeks getting to know each other. Then one day we decided to skip out on school and spend the whole day together. We did. We spent most of that day in bed.

I remember that day well. However, I don't recall it as a day of conquest but as a day of acting without honor. You see that teenage girl was a virgin and she gave herself to me. Her middle name was Iris. In Spanish, Arco Iris means rainbow — something beautiful. Moments after she had given something so precious of her self, she asked me if our lovemaking meant we would someday marry.

Without much thought or sensitivity, I replied, "I'm sure somebody will marry you."

That was a street-kid's answer, totally foolish, immature, and unfeeling. Hey, what did it matter? I just put another notch on my belt!

That street kid has since grown up and as I look back at that day, I'm ashamed. Obviously, neither one of us was ready for what we did that day.

Holding a girlfriend's hand was a big thing for me when I was a teenager. Maybe it went back all the way to when I started school and they made us line up before class in the first grade, two-by-two, holding hands and staying with your partner. Holding hands made you feel safer. Boys and girls always held each other's hands – never boy with boy but girl with girl was OK, according to the nuns who taught at my school.

I held my girlfriend's hand for several reasons. I wanted to show off. Oh Yeah, I'm her guy and she's my girl. She belongs to me! I always wanted to make my girlfriends feel good about our relationship by my showing that we were a couple, going steady, dating. Holding hands was the sure sign that we were exclusive and I wanted everyone else to know it. Holding hands was a proclamation of love, L-O-V-E. Not! Holding hands was a way of working my way to another notch on my belt.

As a teenager, I dated many girls, some younger and some older. Some were two years younger than I was and some were as much as six years older. Nonetheless, did my dating the same girl for a couple of weeks mean anything? Get a grip – NO WAY FOR JOSÉ!

I wasn't ready to settle down; I was just a kid. There was schoolwork to do and all I had was a part-time job at the corner candy store. I had to think of establishing a career first before anything else. I needed to concentrate on important stuff. Dating girls, many girls, was just part of my transition from being a kid to being a man. My sense of commitment to any relationship rarely lasted more than a few hours, at best.

I'd like to thank or blame my father for the shallow mindset about random, meaningless sex that I had as a teenager. Following our parents' divorce, Michael and I didn't see him again until I was nine. Between the ages of nine and twelve, I may have seen my father three times a year. Yet, when I look back at any influence he may have had on my attitude towards girls, his impacts began when he cheated on my mother.

I can still remember one of the last conversations I had with my father. I was about twelve years old and he asked me when was the last time I took a girl out behind the apartment building and made out with her. He also asked, rather graphically, if I had felt her up. He ended with what he considered a necessary pearl of wisdom; "You have to screw as many girls as you can before you get married. Messing around after you get married brings you nothing but trouble." I remember laughing at him. He should have followed his own advice.

I'll be the first to admit that my father set a poor example for meaningful relationships. However, I can't blame him for my actions as a teenager. At the age of five, I knew he had done something wrong, and at twelve, I knew his final advice to me was crude and of no value to me. As a teenager, I knew better; the fault was mine.

Dating for young street guys was a fine art. Allow me to set the stage for you. I dressed sharp. I never went to visit a girl at her house looking like a slob – no blue jeans, or sweatshirts. I was always neat and pressed. I said all the right things to my date's mother and father. If my date invited me to dinner at her house, I always brought

125

flowers or candy for her mother. Mothers ate that stuff up; however, fathers were always skeptical. Fortunately, fathers didn't argue much with the lady-of-the-house. I always made sure I picked up my date on time and delivered her back to her parents at the agreed upon hour. What I planned to do and did, between the pickup and delivery, was hidden from the parents. After all, I was an Altar Boy at my church; I couldn't be all that bad, could I?

During our mid-teen years, many of my friends and I moved into the major leagues; we started taking our dates to clubs for some serious dining, dancing, and drinking. Do you remember my telling you about how easy it was for street kids to walk into a liquor store and buy some booze? Well it was just as easy to walk into such clubs as the Village Gate in Greenwich Village in lower Manhattan, the Manhattan Center in mid-town Manhattan, or the Colgate Gardens, and the Embassy Ballroom in the South Bronx.

I was two months shy of turning sixteen when I took a date to her senior prom and then to the well-known Copacabana in Manhattan. I didn't sneak in; I walked in the front door! We danced and had a few drinks and finished the night listening to Frankie Avalon singing on stage, "Somewhere, there's a place for us," from the movie, West Side Story.

Older teenagers and adults generally frequented the dance clubs I went to as well. The music was a mix of Jazz and Latin tunes. Hot musicians, artists that played the new Latin Jazz, always crowded the clubs. Tito Puente, Celia Cruz, Charlie and Eddie Palmieri, Willie Colon, and Johnny Colon played alongside some of the older Latin artists like Cal Tjader, Johnny Pacheco, and Mongo Santamaria. The clubs were all late-night spots; the music didn't get hot until 10PM and lasted through the night.

We'd leave the clubs at around three or four in the morning, and then stop at an all-night diner for breakfast or end the evening at one of the many all-night Cuchifrito (Puerto Rican chitterlings) greasy spoons in our neighborhood. We would then take our dates back to their apartments or sneak them into our apartments for a full night together.

Let me take you back to that car accident in 1964 again. The plot of that story gets better when I tell you that I was dating four girls at the same time. I had developed bogus excuses that were good enough to keep two of the girls from making plans for us over the Christmas holidays. However, I still had to deal with the other two. Being the foolhardy, Casanova wannabe I was, I actually planned to be with both of them at a party after we attended Christmas Eve's Midnight Mass. "Bold, Foolish, Self-serving, Horny Chump" would have been a good title for me that night. I never made it to the church that night. Maybe I deserved all that because there were no honorable intentions on my mind that night. I wasn't a lover; I was still an apprentice mechanic just like all the other kids.

Some adults were responsible enough to acknowledge the obvious fact that many of the kids in the South Bronx were sexually active. Fortunately, the kids of my neighborhood had one advantage that few others had. We had a pharmacist that sold condoms to teenagers.

Wait! Stop here! What I'm about to tell you is most definitely not a veiled attempt to advocate teenage sex. Nor is it a prescription for safe sex. The following story is about an individual whom I admired as a teenager and as I got older, I admired him even more. Our pharmacist was a good man and a realist who in his own way tried to do something right.

The year was 1963 and a pharmacist on 174th Street in the Bronx, we called him "Doc," was courageous enough to sell condoms to sexually active teenagers. Why do you think he took such a bold step?

Doc sold the condoms very discreetly – under the counter, so-to-speak. With every sale, we got advice not encouragement. Doc didn't pat us boys on the back and tell us to go conquer all the girls we could. On the contrary, he cautioned us about the risk of teenage pregnancies and sexually transmitted diseases. Doc would also sternly plead with us to respect our partners.

Doc knew that if he were caught selling condoms to teenagers he'd certainly bring the wrath of many parents onto himself. Doc didn't seem to worry about that, he just wanted us kids to protect ourselves.

I can assure you, without question, that if Doc had not sold condoms to teenagers, the lives of many of us kids on 174th Street would be very different today. Doc saved lives and our futures. The facts were that of the hundreds of boys and girls I knew only a handful of them were not in some sort of teenage, puppy-love relationship. I can also assure you, dozens of those boys and girls were sexually active. Yet, I know of only one teenaged couple from 174th Street who experienced an unplanned pregnancy. Thanks Doc!

Well here you are, as I once was, a young teenager in love. What do you really know about these new feelings? Mother Nature doesn't send e-mail out to any kid crossing over into puberty. She's actually playing a nasty trick on you early in your life; she's made your blood boil over the opposite sex and you can't explain what's happening to you. You've been given only some of the ingredients of life and yet, somehow you've convinced yourself that that's enough. It's absolutely everything you think you need to know to go out and find love. Sorry ladies and gentlemen, boys and girls and children of all ages – it's not!

OK, let's stop here and take a few minutes for a Love survey. You need to find a good dictionary. Better yet, get several dictionaries and look up these five words: Love, Compassion, Empathy, Commitment, and Truth. I'm confident that you found several and sometimes confusing meanings for each word among the different dictionaries. If you write down the meanings of each of those words on a separate piece of paper, you'll have about fifty pieces of paper. Put all of those notes in a large container and shake them up.

Now go ask some mature friends or members of your family to pick a piece of paper from the container and explain its importance and significance as it may relate to relationships between people.

You're in for a surprise. You won't get 100% agreement among the adults. Each person will have his or her own set of values or levels of importance when it comes to what they feel are significant in personal relationships.

Love has a foundation, a support structure that is built upon over time. The mature contributions that two people pour into that foundation is what gives love its meaning and its strength. Mechanical sex doesn't have a foundation nor does it require meaning. That's what makes the difference between love and mechanics.

Your body's physiological changes during puberty set into motion the capabilities to make babies. However it's time, maturity, and wisdom that prepares you to change a physical act into something meaningful. Don't be fooled into thinking that there's such a thing as a fourteen or fifteen-year-old stud or a sweet sixteen amorous goddess who is ready for love. Your body may be ready for sex; but are your heart, mind, and soul ready for love?

Girls, you are not much different from boys in your desire to explore adult things. The pressure to answer the desire to spend some time with a guy, especially a guy whom you find interesting, attractive, or worst yet, challenging is great. "Do I give myself to this one guy or wait for some guy that I might meet in the future? Is waiting worth the wait? How will I know when it's the right time?" What an awesome set of questions to answer at such an early age.

Only time and maturity can help you find the answers to those very difficult and deeply individual questions. Give yourself the time to prepare for the questions and the answers. Many kids feel that their high school years are a great time to "practice" sex. Remember, that while you may think that practicing sex is the thing to do, you can't practice having dignity and self-respect. Those are precious gems you develop, gems you own. Don't give them away in the name of practice.

I don't believe there is a single answer to the teenage realities Doc, the pharmacist on 174th Street, tried to respond to by selling condoms, at least not from an external source. The one sure source for an answer I know of is within you. You need to decide for yourself when you're ready to give yourself to another. I don't mean when you think you're ready. No! It must be when you know you're ready to take that significant step in life. It would be great to be able to look back at that moment in your life and recall it with a smile and know that it indeed was a wonderful and meaningful moment.

"If you are patient in one moment of anger, you will escape a hundred days of sorrow."

Chinese Proverb

"Nothing in this world is more dangerous than sincere ignorance and conscientious stupidity."

Dr. Martin Luther King, Jr.

Chapter Ten
The Curse of Violence

As a young, street kid, El Barrio taught me something very important; you didn't run away from a fight. Nope, you stood your ground! If some punk got in your face and he was bigger, faster, and meaner or just plan stupid, you took him on. You had to put on the best fight you could and hope that you got some licks in before you really got hurt. Usually, the older kids would stop the fight and the bully would be pulled off the weak and beaten kid. The point wasn't necessarily who could beat whom; kids had to show he or she had "heart."

I have to impress upon you that the concept of stand you ground was O.K. in El Barrio in the 1950's. Back then you got into a fistfight, got a bruised lip or a black eye and the deed was done; the fight was over. Today, fistfights are rare. If you stand your ground, regardless of the neighborhood you live in, you're liable to be hit by a bullet and not a fist. That really scares me.

The first real fight I can remember being in took place on 112th Street in Manhattan. I couldn't have been more than six or seven years old, when a group of men from the block thought it would be a good idea to teach some of us boys the fundamentals of boxing. I remember lacing up a pair of big gloves; they were heavy but I managed to hold them on. The next thing I knew I was standing in front of another kid, staring at his big gloves, and then we were told to start swinging. Frankly, I think the men just wanted to have some fun at our expense.

Well swing we did and, as luck would have it, I caught the first blow right to my glass nose. I kept swinging until I was picked up from behind by one of the men. He held me high enough to be out of reach from the other kid. I think they stopped the fight in order to keep me from bleeding all over the gloves. That was my first fight. Obviously, I had a lot more to learn about fighting. Lesson number one was protecting your nose!

Earlier in the book, I told you about my working the bars as a little kid, shining shoes. One of the many things I learned in those bars was how to smell trouble brewing. I developed a sense of when the conversations were turning into arguments. Those were the times when I would look up from the shoes I was shining and check out the attitudes that went along with the loud voices. I learned to sense anger turning into rage. When rage came, it was time to beat feet. Get the heck out of there! I didn't care if I had finished shining my customer's shoes. Chances were my customer was either going to get into the fight or leave the bar. Trust me; I was out the door pronto!

Self-defense is a natural response and understood in most societies; but what about just plain dumber-than-dirt, act-before-you-think violence? How does a kid react? The answer should be, walk away. Somehow, the lessons from that first bloody boxing match and the episodes in the bars didn't stick with me very long. When I was a little kid, I didn't back away when someone got in my face and I didn't back away years later when I was in high school.

Imagine being a thirteen-year-old freshman and being stabbed just because you're standing in someone's space. That's how my next most memorable fight started; I stood in a guy's space, gave him some attitude, and he stabbed me. Obviously I didn't read the rage in his face fast enough to defend myself. He hadn't even said a word to me. Yet, there I was with blood covering my groin. Let me tell you that at first, I felt violated then I felt the pain, and then the blood started flowing.

I was stabbed in the lower groin, approximately three inches away from my penis. So, let me ask you, should I have backed away before things got out of hand? You bet, considering what I almost lost. However, you'd think that somewhere between being six and thirteen I would've learned better. You're right, I should've; but I didn't!

I was the dummy that heard gunfire and wanted to see where it was coming from. "Hey stupid; when you hear gunfire, you're supposed to beat feet in the opposite direction. If you're in a club, a movie or a gym, hit the ground!" Stupid me, it took a while before I learned to walk away from violence.

My friends didn't think of me as stupid, they thought I was brave. I was known as a person that you didn't want to mess with. I didn't earn that reputation because I had beaten up on anybody or because I was some kind of tough guy. My reputation was solely based on my never backing away from a fight. Stupidity rules!

What made me stop being so stupid? That answer is simple. Imagine seeing someone being hit with a baseball bat right across the forehead. What do you think happens? I don't have to imagine what happens; the memory is still very vivid in my mind. The kid's head popped like a watermelon hitting the ground. You guessed it; he died! Right there in front of the rest of us dummies fighting over something I can't remember. That's what made me stop. Seeing that kid die taught me to walk away.

Thugs must be able to look into another set of eyes, the eyes of their victim's mother and father. I often thought about what my mother's eyes would look like if I were someone's victim. Violence results in profound sadness. I learned to walk away.

The title of this chapter is "The Curse of Violence." There's a definite difference between self-defense and violence. Self-defense is what we did as kids and young adults to protect ourselves. Violence is what you do to others when you stop being human and revert to inhuman instincts. Sadly, in the heat of many battles, we had a tendency of ignoring the difference. I saw too much of that in Spanish Harlem and other parts of New York City when I was young.

I was in my mid-thirties the last time I hit anyone. A twenty-five year old man pushed my teenaged daughter and was about to hit her. My reaction was immediate. I reverted to my New York, street kid mentality – beat them until they stop moving.

I beat that punk with my bare hands until his knees buckled and he couldn't stand. I beat him until my knuckles were raw. I held him up and pounded his body as hard as I could and for as long as I could keep him from falling. When I finally let him fall to the ground, he was unconscious and his body was convulsing. There was an awesome rage in me I knew I had to bring under control.

What made me stop? I stopped because I became acutely aware of the fact that with every punch I was one-step closer to killing that man. That's what stopped me! I refused to cross the line from defense of my family over to the side of murder. Beating the man more would've been violence, not self-defense. Fortunately, I knew the difference.

During my years in New York City, I saw more than my fair share of gang fights. I'll even confess that I've been in a few. Moreover, as I look back on those days, I'll tell you that my getting involved in any gang activity was dumber than dirt. Whenever some friends came over to my apartment and asked me to go out with them, my mother would always say, "He, who does it alone, pays for it alone." Equally true – When something is done in a group, the entire group pays.

137

Imagine being six or seven years old and being caught in the middle of a gang fight. Michael, plus four other kids from the block, and I were playing war with the bricks and sticks from the rubble of a burned-out tenement building, right behind our apartment building. We all heard what sounded like fireworks but we didn't pay much attention to what was really going on outside of our war game. It wasn't until I heard my grandmother yelling at us from the apartment window. She yelled that we had to get back to the front of the apartment building immediately. We yelled back that we were in the middle of a game. Then she pointed toward 113th Street and yelled, "Disparo!" gunfire. We all stopped and looked in the direction she was pointing at; there was an all-out gang fight going on and the fireworks were really gunfire. It was time to beat-feet back to 112th Street.

I saw a great deal of violence during my youth, some of it was of the worst kind; violence that is forced upon you by those you trust. I'm speaking about physical and mental violence – rape, assault, physical injury, and mental or emotional trauma.

When I first considered presenting this topic to you, I thought of how I might present statistical data versus personal experiences. I hate statistics; I'll just continue to present what I know – people hurt people, grownups hurt other grownups, and grownups sometimes hurt children too. I truly feel it's the worst kind when the violence comes from someone you know. I need to share something with you.

I must have been around eight or nine years old when I, unknowingly, found myself in a very dangerous situation. A friend of my family, an older man who lived in my neighborhood, saw me playing with my friends outside my apartment building and approached me. He said he wanted to teach me how to swim. I remember thinking how odd that was; I had never spoken to the man about swimming, yet here he was offering lessons. He then asked me to follow him to his apartment. I had never heard my family speak against this man so I assumed he was an O.K. person. I followed him to his apartment.

Once inside, he offered me a soft drink. I declined; I was eager to hear about swimming. I remember him telling me about some very basic swimming techniques he had learned as a seaman in the Merchant Marines. It was then that he asked me to follow him to his bedroom. Once there, he asked me to take off some of my clothes – he told me that it would be easier to learn some of those techniques he knew if I laid on the bed. That's when the alarms started to go off in my head.

I may have been a kid, but I knew that being in the apartment of someone, whom I knew very little about, wasn't necessarily safe. However, this person was a friend of the family, why worry. He's O.K. isn't he? I took off my shoes, shirt, and pants and I lay on the bed just as he asked. The alarms, however, were still going off in my head.

The next thing that happened made the alarms ring as if it were a four-alarm fire – he took off his pants and he laid on the bed right next to me. I may not have been paying enough attention to the alarms in my head up to that moment, but it was time to snap out of the — It's O.K., he's a friend of the family – stupidity, and beat feet out of there.

I jumped out of the bed, put on my clothes and ran for the door. I was lucky, damn lucky; he didn't try to stop me. I made it out safely and the man never spoke to me again.

I made a few mistakes that day. I didn't listen to the alarms in my head; believe me, those mental alarms are there to protect you. Worst yet, I failed to take any action. I didn't go home and tell my mother or any other family member about the weird stuff that I had experienced. Those were two very big mistakes. I know they were big mistakes because years later I learned that there was a large number of young kids, boys and girls, whom weren't as lucky as I was. I swore, to myself, that I would listen to the alarms and keep myself out of harms way.

You must think of yourself as someone of great value, someone special. You can't let anyone take that away from you – and I mean ANYONE! Regardless of the influences any person may have on your life, be they your parents, brothers, sisters, distant cousins, or Saturday-night date, sexual abuse is violence and VIOLENCE IS WRONG! Don't let their age, height, weight, charm, money, influence, big shot status, or the fact that they're your sweetheart lead you to accept anything less than total respect. Don't ever accept abuse from another human being on this earth – Ever! You are someone special. Report abuse.

Violence among teenagers today says plenty about the value many young people place on their lives and the lives of others. I'm sure you'll agree that's a very sad statement about America's youth. Damn sad!

You've all heard the tragic news about Columbine High School in Colorado. Some of you may have seen the videos on television of students running out of the school under the watchful eyes of heavily armed SWAT Team members. That was a sad day for our Nation. The unfortunate truth is that we've had too many sad days in America. Children killing children is a legacy our Nation can do without.

How do we get this violence to stop? Parents, teachers, clergy members, police officers, and politicians don't have the answers. Sociologist and psychiatrist often argue as to the root causes of violence in our schools, but they don't have the answers either. I know I don't have the answers either; however, I think you do.

I really believe that young people can prevent a lot of violence by simply walking away from it. When I say, "walking away," I mean it in the mental and physical senses. Walk away and help other kids walk away too.

Right about now you're probably thinking, "Oh man, are you nuts? Are you the same person that said he never backed down from a fight when he was a kid? You didn't back down then and you expect me to Chicken Out now? No way, man!"

141

Here's a special note for those of you who carry knives or guns to school or to a party expecting to show to your friends just how bad you are. Unless you're ready to look into the eyes of some kid gasping for air while he or she is dying from their wounds and then listen to their last breath leave their body, leave the weapons at home. I know what those last moments of a person's life looks and sounds like. It's a memory I wish I could erase from my mind. I wouldn't wish that experience on my enemies. It's not something I would wish on anyone.

Unless you're ready to spend years in a small cell behind bars while you watch time waste away slowly, leave the weapons at home. Don't be my brother Ralph! I know your life holds greater promise than a jail cell. Walking away is not an act of cowardice it's an act of choosing life. Walk away!

Gang mentality and the consequences of that mentality are no different today than they were in the days of the cave dweller. Too often, when one gang member steps over the line during a confrontation and commits a serious assault on a victim, the other gang members join in and commit similar assaults on others.

"Hey man! That guy took out a knife, so I took mine out. Then my boys took out their knives too. You shank a few of those punks and they won't mess with us again." You might find some street justice in that quotation when you play the scene out in your mind. However, when we played it out in real life it never went down as it did on TV or in the movies. I know; I've been stabbed. Violence leads to more violence.

Let's talk about gang violence and the flavor of the day assault style, drive-by shootings. Drive-bys are an act of violence that has become a common practice in many American cities. Common or not, it's an act of cowardice. Only cowards, like terrorists, hide in moving cars and shoot indiscriminately into a crowd of people. I don't understand how anyone can take pride in shooting innocent men, women, and especially little children. Drive-by shootings are shameful, indecent acts of violence committed by those who have no value for life. Whether you do it alone or in a group, many people will pay a price for the violence. The price the innocents pay is often greater. Walk away!

"Do all the good you can, by all the means you can, in all the ways you can, in all the places you can, at all the times you can, to all the people you can, as long as ever you can."

John Wesley

Chapter Eleven
Some Keys to the Doors

I discussed the concepts I wanted to present to you throughout this book with a very good friend of mine, Colonel Ted Cope, U.S. Air Force. Ted listened very carefully to everything I said and then he formed an analogy of my concepts. He said, "The world presents itself to everyone with a grand view that stretches from horizon to horizon." He went on to say, "If you cut slices into that grand view, every slice would represent an endless series of possibilities available to everyone. Each of us, by virtue of our own imagination, strengths, weaknesses, sense of adventure, inner desires, and action or inaction, will influence just how many of those possibilities will remain available to us."

Ted was quiet for a moment and then continued with another analogy. He went on to say, "Joe, you and I have been in the U.S. space arena for many years. Paint this picture for the kids who read your book: Life is like the test of a new missile. Every missile that's launched must follow a predetermined launch corridor and trajectory. If the missile fails to stay within the parameters, the right attitude, in either the corridor or trajectory, the Range Safety Officer immediately transmits a self-destruct command to the missile. The test ends explosively.

Kids need to understand that getting through their teenage years is probably the toughest test they'll ever face. They also need to understand and accept the simple fact that if they stay within life's corridors and trajectories, they will pass the test. They need to prepare themselves every day for the test that takes many years. Just like missiles off the launch pad, teenagers need to have and maintain the right attitude in order to succeed. Sure it's hard, but it's part of the test."

Having a person like Ted around is great, especially when I have an idea that needs a sanity-check. However, Ted's a deep thinker and I often have to remind him to keep his responses at a level most earthlings can understand.

Ted translated his analogies for me. He said, "Joe make sure you tell them that each of us can be anything we want to be because each of us is pretty much in control of the course our lives take – you pick it, you be it!"

The first literary agent to review the initial draft of this book said it was too, "preachy." He felt that the last thing my readers needed was someone else telling them what they could or could not do. I promise you that's never been my intention. I'll admit that this is one tough chapter to get through. I've done my best to write every line as if I were a teenager, a teenager with the added benefit of knowing what I know now.

That ability, to look back at one's actions with better knowledge or understanding, is called hindsight. There's an old saying, "Hindsight is 20-20," clear and perfect vision. Others call it "Monday morning quarterbacking," flashing re-runs of yesterday's game and second-guessing what would've, should've, or could've been done to make things perfect. I haven't met anyone that hasn't made a mistake throughout his or her life. Nevertheless, there's one fundamental truth about your life; you're in control. That's right. You're in control!

Long after I passed my teen years, I came to realize a certain truth about life – that from the moment, I came to understand the difference between right and wrong, I had truly been responsible for myself. I also realized that since that same moment in time, every act I committed would speak loudly in three key elements as to the value of my life. Allow me to share my definitions of those key elements with you.

The first key element is Character and it is what you are to yourself and to everyone around you. The content of your character represents you and will guide others of similar qualities toward you. Those whose characters are of lesser qualities may shy away from you or be drawn to you as their mentor. You will be the first judge of those qualities every day when you look at yourself in the mirror. Remember that while you evaluate yourself by your intentions, everyone evaluates you by your actions. In everything you do we see what we believe you to be. Take the right steps in order to build a strong character; a character of distinction.

I created seemingly impossible goals for myself as a young man trying to recover from the mistakes I had made and recapture the time I felt I had lost. Fortunately, I had the words of my grandmother in my mind and her spirit in my heart plus the pride my family expressed at every step of my personal growth and achievement. That emotional support kept pushing me forward.

Later in my life, I was smart enough to marry a young woman who recognized and embraced the challenges I would face reaching those goals and who stood firmly by my side.

Knowing I had so many people believing in me sustained me for the longest time and took me past the early crossings of new horizons. However, they couldn't help me climb the highest mountain. I needed something else.

I had to travel many miles before I found that final bit of strength that helped make the seemingly impossible, possible. I found something that I hadn't really lost but I had ignored my missing it. I had gone from New York to Texas, Georgia, Guam, and finally to New Mexico before I found that one source of strength that would support me when I grew weak with doubt and would lift me when I fell. I found an unlimited amount of inner strength when I entered a house of worship.

Hadn't I learned that back in parochial school? The nuns and priest had said it often enough; but it just wasn't the same. I had to search from my heart not just my logical mind. I had to welcome the gifts that had always been available to me if I had only invited goodness back into my life.

I will not make this a go-to-church, get religious book. I will, however, share with you what eventually became the foundation for what I am today – how I work, live, and love. It's simple; it's a mindset of just doing the right thing. Do right! That's it.

Here's where you might challenge me with, "You've got to be kidding! All I have to do to insure I get the most from this life is to 'Do right?' You've brought me all this way, told me story after story, just to tell me – Do right?"

I'm not kidding. When I say, "seek goodness and do right," I mean that you should seek out what is the right thing to do, then do it to the best of your ability. The first is a choice; the second is an action. I'm not going to define what right means. You already know what it means. Anyone who is more than six years old should have a good feel for what is right or wrong. At twelve to seventeen years of age, you shouldn't need any help at all with the definitions of right or wrong.

An important key to establishing your character is your ability to choose the course of action you feel is right. Then you need to take action and do it right. Doing right isn't just about the stuff that interests you. Doing right is what you are.

Wow, that's a kick-butt challenge I just laid before you! Not really. Give yourself more credit than you do; it just seems hard. I have no doubt in my mind and neither should you about your ability to meet the challenge.

Let's start with doing the best you can in your professional life. Your very first profession is education. Regardless of the school year you're in today, you're in the business of getting educated. Doing right in your present profession means doing the best you can in your schoolwork.

I'm not going to challenge you and say that you have to go out and get straight "A's." Just do your best, regardless of the expectations of others, challenge yourself to surpass your own expectations. Hey, I got a few "C's" in school too; but when I did, I knew it was "get tough" time and I had to work harder. My schools didn't make it easy to go from one grade to the next, so I kept my expectations high. Think of school as a job and think of your grades as the pay you get for the work you do. The best work provides the best pay. It doesn't matter if you're shining shoes or launching rockets.

School is not just about passing grades. Doing your best includes doing what's right for the students you go to school with and the teachers who work hard to help you. You even need to do right for the opposing school teams – soccer, baseball, hockey, football, and especially those brainy kids in the computer clubs. Your school days should fill you with memories of friendship and learning, challenges and victories, the times you stumbled and fell, along with the proud feeling of recovering and standing up. Doing your best will fill you with long-lasting memories. Moreover, it is those memories that will cheer you up and help you stand tall throughout the years of your life.

You need to seek goodness and do right at every point in your personal life too. I'm talking about taking care of your Mom and Dad, Sister and Brother, Aunt and Uncle, Grandma and Grandpa – the core of your family. Do the best you can for them. I hope that it's from them that you draw knowledge, wisdom, a sense of family character, and the standard by which to measure yourself.

I've already shown you how imperfect a family can be; my parents certainly wouldn't win any prizes. However, I still treasure the golden nuggets of wisdom that I got from family members. You do right for them by listening, listening with all your senses, not just your ears.

Consider this; you can't hear anything while you're talking. When I ask you to listen with all your senses, I mean just that. Use your eyes – see what they say with the emotions coming from their bodies and especially their eyes. Use your ears – hear the passion in their words, hear their gentleness and hopes for the future. Use your skin, that's right, your skin – feel their joy as well as their sorrow when you hug them or merely hold their hands. Do right by listening and learning from them.

You also need to seek goodness and do right when it comes to your friends as well as the new kids you meet. Try to maintain a focus on the influence you have on your friends – boys and girls alike. Think hard about what your friends mean to you. Friends are part of you in more ways than you can imagine and you are part of them too. Throughout your life, true friends will become your second family.

When you seek goodness among friends, you choose a select group of boys and girls from the many kids you know. Choose those you feel can be trusted with your life. "Friends don't let friends drive drunk!" You may have heard that saying in TV commercials. It's true. Friends don't let friends put themselves in positions that may hurt them. Friends take care of each other.

I told you about my pothead friends. They weren't friends; they didn't really care about me. They were just kids I hung out with on my block. There must be an unbreakable bond of trust between you and your friends. Trust that you will look after each other's well being and do whatever is necessary to keep each other out of harm's way. Friends won't lie to each other or take advantage of one another. Moreover, they will always expect the best from one another.

Regardless of our age, we all seek to fit in comfortably with the people and the environment wherever we go. I guess it's a universal mindset – fitting in is a necessity. However, many young adults tend to concentrate on and, in turn, shape their identities according to external and physical features. Whatever happened to being attracted to people and places according to their character? Should hyped-up attributes such as athletics, academics, hair and clothing styles, sex, no sex, religion or not, truly define you or your world?.

Let me tell you a story about a 13-year old kid and his attempts at fitting into a new environment. I was a freshman at Aviation High School in Queens, New York in 1962. Wow, that was a long time ago! Some of you may think it was the Dark Ages. Well it wasn't, and I'll bet that 9th grade is no different today than in was in 1962, especially if you're the shortest kid in the entire school. That's right, you guessed it, I was the shortest kid in the entire student body of over 1500 boys and I stood out as if somebody had painted a sign on my back that said, "Please pick on me, kick me, punch me or just make as much fun of me as you can." Freshmen year was not necessarily a great year for me. Moreover, sophomore year wasn't much better either. Sure, I was a bit taller in the 10th grade, but I was still shorter than all my classmates.

I knew that my being the runt of the class meant that I would find myself in a few arguments and probably a fight or two. I didn't let anyone push me around and whenever I was challenged into a fight, I wasn't smart enough to back down. Consequently, I learned quickly during the 9th grade that I needed to find some big friends if I wanted to survive. The bigger and meaner my choice of friends was, the better. Fortunately, after some of the punks in the class realized that I wouldn't back down they usually decided to move on to other targets. Besides, my big friends were always around to suggest that it would be wise to leave me alone.

I remember one incident in my 10th grade aircraft engine class when a dude named Glenn Skaggs (yes, I still remember his name) picked me up by my overalls. With my feet dangling off the floor, he

153

pulled my face close to his and said, "I'm going to kick your ass." I believed him.

As surprised as I was, I remember staying very calm and saying to him, "I suggest you put me down before my friends see what's going on." Too late, several of my bigger friends were already standing behind me.

My feet were still off the ground when one of my friends told Glenn, "Put him down now or we'll take turns hurting you." My feet found the floor again. Soon after that incident, my days of having fistfights on my way home ended.

So, what does that have to do with fitting in? I think the answer lies in what I did to get to a point where the majority of my concentration was on academic studies instead of self-defense.

When other students picked on me, I stood my ground. Sadly, I recognize that in today's supposedly more advanced society, standing your ground in the 9th grade can cost you your life. Today, I would probably stand my ground differently, probably by avoidance rather than confrontation, by thinking first and then reacting. I'd try to talk-it-out or just walk away. In whatever fashion I choose I would refuse to become like them.

The same is true for the way those "big" classmates became my friends. The "runt" kid, me, just talked to my fellow students as I would to anyone else. I let people get to know me and I made every effort to get to know them. Whenever I found a class subject or project my classmates needed help with, I gave that help freely and without any expectation of payback. I made friends my way.

If you compare my junior high school and high school days to yours, you'll see many similarities. We had the sense of needing to fit in just as you have today. In the sixties, most of the boys in school had long hair. Blame it on the Beetles, Sly and the Family Stone or other rock groups of that era; but long hair was the rave, except in my house. I was a pimple-faced kid with skin so oily you could fry an egg on my forehead; right after you finished playing connect-the-dots with all my pimples – Gross! Who needed long hair? I stood out enough already.

Bell-bottomed jeans, tie-dyed shirts, and sandals were a rave too; again, not in my house. My mother couldn't afford such clothes nor would she ever have allowed me to wear them even if she had the money.

Smoking cigarettes between classes and wearing as outrageous an outfit as you could get away with was the school scene in the '60s. However, I dressed very conservatively: slacks, shirts, sweaters, shoes. I didn't get up every morning, stand in front of my closet, and pick out clothes that would make a statement. I merely picked out whatever I liked wearing, something comfortable and still within the limits.

I even tried smoking as a way to fit in; but that didn't do anything for me. All the boys would practice holding their cigarettes and try to mimic every fancy inhaling and exhaling trick the television and movie stars were doing on the screens. There were too many things to do in order to fit in at school. Frankly, I thought it was a waste of energy then and I still do today.

155

It wasn't until I was in my early twenties that I came to a realization that changed my way of thinking. Allow me to suggest this to you that there's no place on Earth where you don't belong simply because you don't "fit in." You belong wherever you are and wherever you want to be. Don't let anyone tell you otherwise. Don't let anyone's fears, attitude, or ignorance convince you that unless you look, act, or think like them you don't belong. When you hear that stuff and believe it, you've sunk lower than the people who've made you feel that way.

I heard, "You don't belong here," too often on the streets of New York when I was a kid; but I didn't listen. Ignorant people, lopsided attitudes, and even my own insecurities would try to convince me I wasn't "worthy" or "good enough" to walk through certain neighborhoods of the City. I assure you, I wouldn't be where I am today if I didn't finally come to the realization that I belong in any place I go and so do you. We don't have to prove anything to anyone else.

I'm going to take a giant leap from my high school days to the present and share a story with you about another thirteen-year old boy; a story I feel you can readily connect with.

My wife and I celebrated our 34th wedding anniversary at the Wigwam Resort in Litchfield, Arizona, just outside of Phoenix. We arranged for our three daughters, my son-in-law, and all our grandchildren to be there with us for a 4-day weekend. Over dinner one evening, my thirteen-year-old grandson mentioned that he wanted to bleach the hair on the crown of his head blond. When I asked him why, he shyly answered, "To fit in."

Why would a boy of thirteen want to go to an extreme of bleaching part of his jet-black hair blond? Is fitting in the universal answer? My initial response to his seemingly awkward answer was, "Not in my lifetime!" As the conversation went around the table from his parents to his aunts, my grandson only heard negative comments from the family. I then cut the conversation short by asking, "Why do you have to fit in with the other kids at school? Why can't they fit in with you? Better yet, why does anyone have to change their own style for the sake of fitting in?"

My wife, being a gentle soul and an outstanding grandmother, spoke before my grandson could answer my questions. She said, "He'll do whatever his parents allow him to do. He doesn't live in our household and he only has to conform to his parents' wishes."

As we said our good byes before we left on our separate routes back to our homes, I hugged my grandson and gently said, "I love you. If you feel you have to change, change because you feel it is right for you. Don't change just to fit in." Months later, his hair was still, jet-black. I was glad to find out from my daughter that my grandson made the decision all on his own.

I felt I needed to share that story with you in order to emphasize that each of you is unique. Without question, each of you has extraordinary, one-of-a-kind gifts. Don't mask those gifts by mimicking the internal or external traits of others. If you're to be appreciated for your extraordinary gifts, let them show in their own colors. Choosing an identity or a style is yours to choose and yours to create. Give yourself the opportunity to create a style as unique as you know you are. Create it as you turn the pages of your book, the book that will be your life.

Taking care of your family and your friends is an absolute necessity if you're going to take care of the next person I'm going to talk about – You.

For too long a period in my life, I didn't take care of myself very well. I had picked too many wrong paths and nearly destroyed any hopes of a future. I kept ignoring what should have been obvious – every step I was taking was screwing up any chance of my fulfilling any of my goals and dreams. I seemed to care less and less about what people thought of me. I didn't listen to my family or to my friends. I couldn't care less about where I was or where I might end up. My future; what future was there? I couldn't even see past the end of my nose.

Please don't go down the path I did. There's absolutely no reason for you to do that. If you've already started down that path, take a good look in the mirror. The "you" that you see will not be the same tomorrow; the view will be much worse. I pray that you will never see your face in the mirror as I once did – bloody, swollen, stitched, and scarred.

Only you can turn around from the path you're going down – and you must turn around. If you feel as though you've gone too far to turn back now, stop the whining, get some help, and get your stuff together. Don't sell yourself short. You can do it. Do it now! Take care of yourself. There is only one you, so do right by yourself.

All of my personal relationships are founded on the exchange of respect between the other person and me. If I admire you, I obviously respect you. If I listen to your advice, I obviously respect you. If I call you friend, I obviously respect you. And, if I say I love you, I obviously respect you. Your respect should not be a mystery to those you admire, seek counsel from, or call friend. They should see that respect from you in every way.

Consider the following questions. Would you let one of your friends come into your parents' home wearing mud-covered running shoes and track dirt into the house? Would you let that friend jump on your parents' living room furniture and plop those muddy shoes on the coffee table?

If your answer to either of those questions is "Yes," then I don't want you or your friend to darken my doorstep. Why? You don't deserve to be invited into my house. You don't have the right to disrespect anyone's property or to encourage anyone else to do so. I don't have the right and certainly, no one else does.

Let me ask you, what if your mother were present when that Muddy-Buddy friend of yours happens to invade and insult her house. Would you let your friend respond to your mother's complaints with foul and abusive language? I hope your answer to that question is a loud, "No!" If you had to think twice about your answer, I certainly don't ever want you in the presence of my mother or any of my family elders.

You don't have the right to disrespect anyone, family member, friend or stranger, or to encourage anyone else to do so. Moreover, no one, certainly not that Muddy-Buddy, has the right to disparage your character with crude behavior.

Tell me, do you have the right to be abusive, physically or verbally, to all those different kids in school? You know those tall or short, fat or skinny, HOT or not so pretty, brainy or nerdy, poor or rich, other side of the tracks, foreign kids you see every day and you have a personal itch about accepting them for whom they are? You know you don't!

Hey, you may have been the object of someone else's abuse in the past, so now it's time for payback, right? Wrong! You don't have the right! Remember who those kids are. They are the sons and daughters, brothers and sisters of other people. You really don't have the right. Nobody does. No way, no how!

I recognize that this is hitting some of you right between the eyes. That's life in the Big City, tough it out! I don't like seeing kids disrespecting other kids. Such behavior opens you up to accepting what should be unacceptable. Remember that you too can be a target of such abuse. Do Right. Respect is a critical part of your Character.

Let me ask you to conduct the following test for a period of only two days. There's very little you have to do. The test calls for you to use one of two words and then you really need to pay attention to the response you'll get from everyone you say those words to.

The rules of the test are that on Day-1 you use these words with anyone that is more than five years older than you are. On Day-2, use these words with everyone your age or older. You will ask or answer every question and every greeting using one of these two words at the beginning or end of you responses. You must use the words with everyone you speak to — family, friends, neighbors, and strangers alike (according to the rules for day-1 and 2). The words are Sir and Ma'am.

Hey, I'm not asking you to do this so that I can prove a point. However, if you use those two uncompromising words and pay attention to the reaction from those who hear you say those words, you will immediately begin to understand how simple respect will change your life.

I was watching "The Late Show with David Letterman" recently and he had five teenagers from different parts of the United States on the show displaying their science projects. Only one of the five teenagers, a young man from the Southeast, answered Mr. Letterman's questions with the word "Sir" in his responses. Mr. Letterman stopped the show and asked the audience what they thought of this young man's manner of speaking to his elders. I remember the audience applauding and Mr. Letterman saying, "You're a fine young man. Your parents have raised you right." Think about that for a moment. Think about how you would feel if you were that young man, in the spotlight for using one simple word reflecting respect.

Don't think of your using Sir or Ma'am only as acts of humility and respect. Yes, they are that; but they are also a way for you to set the standards for the manner in which you expect to be treated. When you give it, you deserve it, and should expect it too. This you have the right to do. You have the right to expect respect when you give respect.

Now, if the test goes as I predict it will, what's to stop you from using this concept every day as a means of growing? The reason I insisted you pay close attention to the manner in which your simple signs of respect – Sir/Ma'am – has on people is for you to use what you see, the reactions of others, as a means of growing. Believe it; you'll make people take notice of you.

Once you've captured their attention, then it's time for you to show your stuff. You've opened the door with respect, now show them your other great qualities. You'll attract good people. Moreover, those good people will bend over backwards to help you succeed.

Finally, respecting yourself is critical and in doing so, you will grow up a better you. Remind yourself every day that you need to respect what you do, how you do it; why you do it; and with whomever you do it. Think about what I'm about to share with you and then share it with those around you – "Respect is the biggest force that will drive your success and it is the foundation of Character."

The second key element is Future; it is what you will be at the end of the day. Either you will have set yourself in motion to become the person you want to be tomorrow and in years to come or you will have remained the same as you were yesterday. By your actions, you will have opened or closed the doors of opportunity. You can't waste your days; don't waste your steps. Try your best to move forward.

Over the years, I've had the opportunity to speak to many groups of schoolchildren, several from inner-city environments, and I've often shared with them some of the same stories I've shared with you. I try to end every session with a discussion about achieving personal goals, reaching across the broad expanse of oceans and crossing over horizons just to learn about what was on the other side.

I talk to the kids about those few square city blocks I thought of as my "world" when I was young. Somehow, at an early age I sensed that if I wanted to expand my world I'd have to change. I would have to build upon what I had already learned and use it to explore the unknown.

I've already told you about the twist and turns my teenage years took; but what did I use to build a bridge to the future I had envisioned? You might hate the answer. It's a one-word answer – "Education." I made education a priority in my life.

Here's another piece of reality, you can have a Doctorate degree and choose to flip burgers at the corner burger shop for the rest of your life. Flipping burgers is an honorable job. I know; I flipped a few in my early years. Earning a Ph.D. and flipping burgers is a personal choice. Believe me when I tell you that if you don't get a good education you won't get to make the choices. If you fail to get an education, someone else will make your career choices for you. Don't give anyone else the right to define your life's work.

Please allow me to go one-step further. I believe it was the Chinese philosopher Confucius who said, "Choose an endeavor that you love and you'll never have to work a day in your life." I think Confucius was trying to say that you should study what interest you. Study those things that create a passion in you – a passion to learn even more. Then go off and do what you love and you will love what you do for your entire career.

There are several essential factors in my life that I credit for my successful career. My education is one of the top factors. A good education helps open doors. The more complete your education is, the easier it will be for you to open the doors and seize those opportunities that will help you realize your goals.

You might be thinking, "Wow, that's easy for you to say Mister. Can you back it up?"

You bet I can. Here's a piece of history I didn't share with you earlier – I'm a high school dropout. I dropped out of school two months before my senior prom. Why would I quit school when I was so close to graduation? The excuses were many but none was a viable reason for putting my future into reverse gear.

One day I just stopped going to school. I hid the fact well from my mother, until she received a notice from the school stating that I was absent twenty-four days in the semester. The note also said I was expelled. My mother didn't ask me where I had been during those twenty-four days and I didn't offer any explanations. Nevertheless, I was done with school and I had to move on with my life.

Getting on with life meant finding a job. A serious job with a reasonable salary; I couldn't live with my mother forever. I needed a job with some sense of promise, plus medical and dental benefits. I needed a job that would substitute as the viable reason for my having quit school. Well the cold and cruel world slapped me hard across the face when all I could find were jobs as a grocery store clerk, a grill cook at a burger joint, a soda jerk at an ice cream parlor, or a delivery-boy for a messenger service in midtown Manhattan.

Talk about a rude awakening. That little piece of paper, called a diploma, was necessary for any job paying more than minimum wage. I had nobody to blame but myself for my sorry state of affairs.

Most of my friends were either finishing high school or enrolled in college classes. Meanwhile, I spent my days at my no-promises, no-benefits, nothing to brag about jobs. Nobody understood why I dropped out of school. My family chalked it up as another sign of irresponsibility on my part. Well I can tell you that my quitting school wasn't irresponsible, it was just plain stupid. You bet; I screwed up. I screwed up big time.

Luckily, that red-haired girlfriend of mine helped me refocus on what was most important. I started studying again and earned a General Equivalency Diploma (GED). However, that wasn't enough. My stint with jobs of limited potential painted a clear picture for me. A picture I couldn't ignore; I had to earn a college degree.

My GED got me in the door at Chemical Bank in New York, a job with real benefits, including college tuition reimbursement. I used that opportunity to start my college education at the New York Institute of Technology. I busted my butt working a full time job in the evenings and going to school during the day. I made the Dean's Honor List the first semester. Chemical Bank encouraged me to continue going to school when they promoted me to Shift Operations Supervisor of their Broker's Loan Processing Division on Wall Street. That was the first door that opened for me.

I left Chemical Bank to join the Air Force. My military duty made it difficult for me to go to school on a full-time basis; but part-time was better than no time. Therefore, I struggled with the hours and finished my Bachelors Degree in Aerospace Science at the University of Albuquerque. My overall grade point average was 3.4 on a 4.0 basis. Having earned my degree, the Air Force then selected me for Officer Training School (OTS) where I received my commission as a Second Lieutenant. OTS was the second door that opened for me.

I didn't stop there. Two years after completing my BS degree, I completed my Master of Science Degree in Business at the University of Northern Colorado. Within a few years, I added several more academic and professional programs to my resume. More and more doors opened.

What did education really do for me? Consider the following list as a brief summary of what education did for me, and what it can do for you too. I learned to communicate, write, and speak in a concise and effective manner. I've written reports to senior government officials and I've spoken to audiences as large as eight hundred. Surely, I didn't learn to write well enough to publish books on the street corners of the South Bronx.

I learned to use the tools of my chosen profession, Space Operations, through schooling and fieldwork. I learned about teamwork, how to deal with technologies of different countries, engineering, space medicine, and military history. Professional education set the foundation for my future.

I didn't stop my education when I completed formal degree programs. I pursued as many professional development programs as I could. I completed all the Professional Military Education programs available to me as an enlisted man and as an officer: Non-Commissioned Officer Leadership School, Squadron Officer School, and Air Command and Staff College. As a civilian, I honed my skills over the years by earning several certifications that acknowledge my expertise in important areas of my profession. Those certifications have helped me reach new heights in my career.

Education took me from the flight line working on B-52s to the caverns of Cheyenne Mountain where I served as a Missile Warning Officer. I attribute my assignment to one of the Air Force's most prestigious organizations, The Office of the Secretary of the Air Force, to my furthering my education and enhancing my skills. Today, I'm a Strategic Policy Analyst and a consultant to the Department of Defense on Space Operations. That's right, more doors opened!

Education is something no one can take away from me. The more I acquired the stronger the foundation upon which I could build my future and my family's future. I'm confident the same will be said about you.

The third key element is Legacy and that is what you'll leave behind and how you'll be remembered. Each of us will leave behind many things for many people. I don't think of the things that I might leave humankind; that's a bit too aggressive for me. I think in terms of what I'll leave the people I love, the people I work with, and the profession I've worked at for so many years. Much of what defines your legacy comes from what you teach others. The number of times you reach out to help others, the words you use, and the passion behind your words and deeds are part of the teaching you do. I try to mark my steps along a path of commitment and service that I hope will build upon the superior legacies of those who came before me.

I've shared with you many stories about my teen years, too many of which were negative. However, I did have a deep feeling of achievement during my teenage years that has carried on through all my years since. That constant is derived from being proud of my membership in Civil Air Patrol (CAP). CAP is an auxiliary of the United States Air Force and it sponsors aerospace education through a cadet program for thirteen to eighteen-year olds. CAP also has an adult program with two primary missions, members conducting the administration of the cadet program and members directly supporting the Air Force's nationwide search and rescue activities. Both programs are truly interwoven as cadets and senior members participate jointly in search and rescue missions as well as other community service programs.

Up until the day of my car accident, I was an active member of CAP. My cadet activities had filled many weekdays with community service activities. As I look back on those days, I know that I never felt as though the time I dedicated to CAP was wasted. I learned and experienced so many new and diverse things that are still with me today.

I traveled to many military installations aboard Air Force planes as a member of CAP. Especially exciting were the opportunities to see American military life, a radical difference from my inner-city environment. I remember climbing aboard a C-119, an Air Force paratrooper and cargo carrier, that took a plane-load of cadets from Westchester County Airport to Plattsburg Air Force Base, near the U.S. and Canadian border. There I witnessed Strategic Air Command officers and airmen on alert duty.

I've seen many examples of commitment and service over the years since that trip to Plattsburg AFB. However, the memory of those B-47 bomber and KC-135 tanker crews has served as the cornerstone of my commitment and service to my community as well as to my Country. Young men and women, working under the guidance of their senior officers and non-commissioned officers, preparing their airplanes for something they hoped would never happen – an attack upon the United States requiring a nuclear retaliatory strike against the attacking nation.

Over the two weeks that I stayed at Plattsburg AFB, I saw crew members working long hours, on the ground and in the air, every action performed to an interesting tempo and sameness. Everything from their sharp looking airplanes to the sharp creases on their uniforms spoke of pride and professionalism. These were real Americans.

CAP taught me first aid and other life-saving techniques. I credit what I learned in CAP for the skills I used to save a little boy and a young woman from drowning and for being able to provide the right emergency treatment for a teenage girl following a serious fall that broke her back.

Even though I was just 15-years old, the adults that were trying to assist the injured girl stopped and listened to me as I kept them from moving her just to make her more comfortable; movement that would have worsened her injuries. Her parents allowed me to immobilize her neck and arms as well as treat her for shock until paramedics arrived.

I guess it was that sense of service I learned from CAP that motivated me to respond to a fire at my high school. The fire had started in a large utility room and heavy black smoke was coming from beneath the door and filling the hallway. I pulled the nearest fire alarm, ran to the administration office to report the fire's location, and then I grabbed a fire extinguisher as I returned to the scene of the fire. One of the school's maintenance engineers and I entered the room. Each of us had a fire extinguisher and together we put the fire out. By the time the fire department arrived, most of the students had already been evacuated. Only two people suffered any smoke inhalation problems, the maintenance engineer and me. I was 15-years old.

I'm not tooting-my-horn here. Those are some of the good memories from my teenage years. I'm just sharing with you some of the positive things that can happen when you develop a sense of serving others instead of just taking care of yourself and doing your thing.

There are countless community service organizations throughout the United States. If you feel something is missing in your life and you want to do something bigger and better than what you're doing now, getting involved in community service may be the answer. If there isn't something that interests you, don't stop there. Start a service program of your own. Other kids have done it, so can you!

When I think in terms of community service, I'm most often reminded of some of the most simple, yet profoundly generous acts of kindness that I witnessed my grandmother do.

As a kid in New York City during those long-ago 1950s and '60s, the numbers of "street people" was nothing like it is in 2001. When I see men and women standing on street-corners begging for handouts today, I'm reminded of the scenes I had only seen in pictures taken during the Great Depression of the 1920s and '30s. Yes, we had a few street people in the '50s and '60s; however, we had a cruel name for such unfortunate people back then, we called them "Bums."

I don't remember there being more than a handful of bums that hung out on the streets of Spanish Harlem. They were mostly alcoholics, male and female adults; I never saw a teenage bum. These quiet folks relied on the generosity of the neighborhood residents. I can proudly say that the people of Spanish Harlem were generous to those whom were less fortunate.

I must have been about five years old when I first noticed my grandmother placing the leftovers from our dinner in metal containers and then placing the containers in a box. She then added plates, knives, forks, spoons, and napkins to the box. What struck me odd was that she tied the box up with a long rope, opened the kitchen window, which faced the alleyway behind our apartment building, and lowered the box out the window to the alleyway below.

I remember standing next to my grandmother and asking her, what she was doing. She didn't answer me. She just picked me up by the waist and held me tight as she leaned me over the window's ledge so that I could see where the box of food went.

In the alleyway below, there were several men and women; bums carefully distributing the food my grandmother had sent them. I watched them as they ate their food, talked amongst themselves, and laughed at the stories being told. When they finished eating, they called my grandmother's name and when she appeared at the window, they all said, "Muchas gracias Doña Hortensia." My grandmother acknowledged their simple and humble "thank you" as she pulled the rope up, retrieving the box full of dishes.

My grandmother performed that simple act of kindness every day for all the years we lived in Spanish Harlem. I wish I could say that I followed her example and that I've been dedicated to a daily act of giving such as hers; but I can't. However, I will tell you that I started giving food to the needy in my teenage years and I haven't stopped. My wife and I have done it. My children and their children have done it too. Everyone in my family has heard me tell the same story about my grandmother.

Even to this day, when I do something as simple as give a sandwich and a cup of coffee to a street person, I think of Grandma. Muchas gracias Abuelita!

Just think of the simple acts of kindness you can do. I promise you, those acts will fill your spirit and form the foundation of your legacy.

"I'd rather be a could-be if I cannot be an are;
because a could-be is a maybe who is reaching for a star.
I'd rather be a has-been than a might-have-been, by far;
for a might-have-been has never been, but a has was once an are."

Milton Berle

"Tell me not, in mournful numbers,

Life is but an empty dream!

For the soul is dead that slumbers,

And things are not what they seem.

Life is real! Life is earnest!

And the grave is not its goal;

Dust thou art; to dust returnest,

Was not spoken of the soul."

Henry Wadsworth Longfellow

Chapter Twelve

A Tribute to My Heroes

I believe life is survival of the wisest. Beyond the influence of my roots is the influence of the people and events that helped me choose a path, take my steps one at a time, and be mindful that each step I took defined my character, my future, and my legacy.

Yet, I recognize that your present world is different from my "growing up" world. Your parents' world was different and should you have children, the world awaiting them will certainly be different too. Those differences are a universal reality. Change will happen and no, you probably won't have a vote and nobody will ask you for your opinion. All I did, your parents did, and you will hopefully decide to do is deal with it.

One very important thing my brothers and I seemed to ignore as kids in the city was the wisdom our parents were trying to share with us when they tried to tell us what type of kids we should and shouldn't play with. Our parents were pleading with us to consider the paths other kids were taking and judge the merit of what they were doing based on right from wrong.

As Michael and I grew up, so many things were happening to our little worlds that we weren't sure which way to turn. When I look back at those days, I often feel that it would've been great having our dad nearby. Just having someone extra in our lives to keep reminding us that every step we took was another step that could make us or break us. However, we weren't that fortunate. I am not a product of my culture, family, friends, environment, or the greater world around me. I am only a product of the choices I made. You, without question, will be a product of yours.

My hope is that you read this book and recognize that you will be a product of your choices. The steps that you will take throughout life are your choices. I hope you choose wisely. At an early age, most of us understand the concepts of what is right and wrong. We learn those concepts from our parents, families, teachers, neighbors, clergy, and friends. As we develop an understanding of those concepts, we learn that those concepts are based on teachings from our ethnic cultures, religious beliefs, and family traditions. Those teachings help form the foundation of our character.

As we develop that understanding further an inherent inner conscience grows in each of us; an inner-voice that serves us forever.

That inner voice is what provides us the sense that the step we're about to take feels good and is right for us. That inner voice also tries to protect us. We can hear it alerting us that a certain step may bring harm to others and ourselves because it violates our concept of right versus wrong.

I recently visited my family in New York and took a ride down to the beach and I stood at the very same Coney Island shoreline I had visited when I was a kid. I'm fifty-three years old now and the realization I had was of something I hadn't known as a child. I couldn't have possibly imagined that getting beyond that seam which separated the dark Atlantic waters from the blue sky would require the conquering of a lifelong series of challenges. Nor could I have envisioned that in conquering those challenges I would find happiness and rewards beyond my imagination. Most surprising of all was that in my meeting the challenges placed before me, I would define the legacy I would leave for my family.

I looked again, past the Coney Island shoreline, over the water and beyond to the horizon, and I smiled. I know that I no longer need to wonder or daydream; I've been fortunate and blessed. I've been to the other side of that horizon and I've managed to take my children with me. No, they didn't just go along for the ride. They were part of the struggle. They witnessed my wife and me working hard to overcome challenges and reach our goals. It wasn't a free ride for our kids. My wife and I set standards of behavior, for our children, standards they had to meet or exceed. Standards regarding education, an honest work ethic, personal integrity, charity to others, and the tenacity to fight back when they sensed injustice were coupled and strengthened by the ties of family.

My smile disappeared quickly on that day as I turned away from the beach and looked back at what the neighborhood near the beach had become. The rows of pretty bungalows were now shattered shacks, empty lots, or burned-out skeletal remnants of what was once so beautiful. Poverty and despair had set in. Pride had disappeared. The streets were open trash dumps. The empty, weed-infested pits filled with stripped vehicles and broken furniture served as makeshift playgrounds. What happened? This sad reality didn't happen overnight.

I don't have the answers as to what turns a person's life into a dismal state of affairs besides his or her own making. However, I do know what helped me have a clear vision and what gave me the strength to reach and grab hold of my dreams. I know what saved me and eventually carried me across the ocean and beyond many horizons. Some of it came from my heroes.

My first thoughts when the phone rang were that she had died. I was right. The end had come swiftly for my grandmother; at least that's what Victor, my younger brother, told me when he called on Saturday, 14 May 1983 at 2:30AM. He asked me what I planned to do. There was no question as to whether or not I would attend the funeral; I had to be there. I felt as though I had been her last glimmer of hope in life. That hope had come late.

I immediately called an airline and made a reservation for an early flight out of San Antonio, Texas. Once made, I went back to sleep. I felt as if a great fear had been lifted from my mind. As much as we might fear it, death will happen. I had come to expect it with every late night call I received. Her pain and suffering were now gone. I slept peacefully the rest of the night.

I was a Flight Commander at the U.S. Air Force Officer Training School at the time and I had a tremendous set of responsibilities to many people. They would all have to wait until I said this last good-bye to my grandmother. My first stop that morning was the Deputy Commander's house. I explained everything to him. I told him I had already arranged for a substitute instructor who agreed to finish all the paperwork required to commission my students the following Tuesday. He gave me verbal authorization for whatever leave (a military term for authorized absence from duty) time I felt would be necessary. He also assured me that his staff would check in on my family while I was gone.

The flight from San Antonio to New York City was a blur to me. I had arranged for a friend of mine to pick me up at LaGuardia Airport and drive me into Manhattan. I rarely wore my Air Force uniform when I traveled; however, I wore it that day. I wanted to be left alone and oddly enough, most civilian airplane passengers don't often strike up conversations with military people.

I filled the hours in flight thinking about the last time that I had seen my grandmother. I had been in uniform that day too. She had a curious love for that uniform. She liked seeing me in uniform but hated to see the old-style round service hat. The sight of that hat would bring tears to her eyes. I made sure I only wore the more modern, straight-lined flight cap whenever I went to see her.

There had been a late night call two months earlier. My grandmother had suffered a mild heart attack and she specifically asked that I not be told; Victor told me anyway. The doctors felt that a visit from me would help comfort her, so I took emergency leave from duty and went to New York.

I arrived late for visiting hours but was allowed to see her; I wasn't about to take no for an answer. I had traveled too far to wait another day. I sat at her bedside for the longest while. I clearly remember looking at the lines in her face. Time had made its mark on her.

She awoke and was surprised to see me. "¿Por que estas aqui? ¿Quien te llamo?" why are you here and who called you, she asked. "I'm not that sick, and I'm certainly not near death." All I could do was laugh. She was connected to a few monitors and a respirator yet she was as cantankerous as ever. She held my hand and laughed with me. We retold many of the stories we had come to share between us since my childhood.

I spent a few days in New York, mostly in the hospital with her. Each day she assured me she was well and that all she had suffered was a minor setback in her way of life. She promised to go slow and get plenty of rest. The doctors also assured me that with a more subdued lifestyle she still had a few years left in her.

Before I left New York, I dropped by to see her on my way to the airport. She was upset that none of her other six grandchildren had come to see her or had even bothered to call and ask about her condition. She said that someday, they too would know of the hurt she was feeling. Her eyes filled with tears. I embraced her and asked for her blessing. We shared one last story and our last laugh.

That was March 1983. I knew that I had spoken to my grandmother, Doña Hortensia De la Rosa, for the last time.

I arrived in New York City late in the afternoon and went directly to the funeral parlor. A very somber man escorted me to the room where my family had gathered. I entered the room and could hear several people ask others about who I was and I heard the whispered answers, some of which were wrong. I spotted the casket and went directly toward it. A few feet away, Aunt Virginia was reciting the rosary; something she had done for many members of our family.

I knelt beside the casket for just a few moments. I thanked God for the peace my grandmother had now finally found. The lines in her face were still there. She was dressed in pink; a color I had never seen her wear. The dress had a lace collar and cuffs. I looked at her hands; they still looked strong. The same hands that I had watched cook, mend, cure, punish wrongs, and gently hold those that were in pain. An age, an era, a way of life had now passed. I wanted to scream and tell the world about this terrible passing.

Having said my prayers, I stood up and turned to greet my family. Several people were watching me, following my movements around the room. I knew most of the faces, many of which I hadn't seen in years. When I saw my mother sitting on a nearby couch, I walked up to her, embraced her, and asked for her blessing. Then I whispered the traditional, "Te acompaño en su dolor," I accompany you in your pain. She gave me her blessing and asked about my wife and children. She understood that they wouldn't be able to attend the funeral.

The rest of the evening was taken up in prayer and in meeting relatives that were distant to me by either time or blood. I found it almost comical that the only times I had seen such large family gatherings was either at a wedding or a funeral. There were those in the crowd who were there to fulfill the obligatory ritual of the wake, so as not to insult the elders of the family. Others were shedding tears in earnest sorrow for a true loss. Some mourners present were feeling the loss of their Gibraltar, the rock that they could always depend on to be there when they were in need. Well tonight that zero-interest, no-hassle bank was officially closed. The Chief Loan Officer was dead.

I was introduced to one of my grandmother's younger brothers. I had never met Don Baldomero De la Rosa and as he stood up from his chair, he examined my uniform and then looked into my eyes as he put his hand out as if to shake my hand. Instead of taking his hand, I embraced him and asked for his blessing. He kissed my check and gave me his blessing.

There were some people missing; Michael was one of them. He was the one who Grandma had said would someday feel the pain of being left alone. She had had her greatest hopes in him. He was to be the chosen one who would lead the family in years to come. She took to her grave the knowledge that many of her dreams would never happen; the faded dreams of the Matriarch.

The burial was set for Monday morning; I made plans to return to Texas immediately after the services. I had no desire to remain and mourn publicly. Those who were important to me understood; the opinion of those that weren't didn't matter.

My cousin, Salvador Alonso, Jr., arrived from his duty station in time for the services. We exchanged salutes as soon as he saw me. Some of the family thought it odd; but the Army had taught him well that, cousin or not, sergeants salute officers. The salute served the purposes of his acknowledging my military rank and our joining in this sad day's affair. We both understood that. Following the internment, I went directly to the airport.

My grandmother's death marked the end of an era. She had been a very wise woman who nurtured her family as best she could. Most often, it was her insightful counsel that would be her greatest gift to everyone. I recall one of her many truisms; "Your reach is only limited by your vision." She said that often to me, especially in my teenage years as she saw me floundering, trying to find a path. If only more members of my family had listened to her. I wish more of my friends could have heard her too. She had wonderful insights on what lay beyond the horizon. She was also one of my greatest heroes.

Where do you find your heroes today? Where are the people whose traits you want to emulate? Do you select your heroes from a list of popular athletes or the rich and famous? Are your heroes on TV or in the movies?

What did I look for in my heroes? What was it about them that influenced me so much that I wanted to be like them? Did I seek perfection in them? Did I insist that they be religious, well educated, or even good-looking? Did they have to be my friends' heroes too? So many questions and so many filters we can use to select our heroes.

Well, I don't know about you, but I didn't find my heroes among any of those popular groups. Yes, there were good people, famous "stars" and athletes, around when I was a kid. Mickey Mantle and Roger Maris of the New York Yankees; Meadowlark Lemon of the Harlem Globetrotters; Major John Glenn, United States Marine Corps, the first American to orbit the earth – all good men! Did I find my heroes among those public figures? No, I found my heroes among ordinary people, people I knew well, and even among people whom I met only briefly.

Felix, Jimmy, Michael, and I spent equal amounts of time in each other's homes, meeting relatives and quite often, hearing unique pieces of wisdom and advice from the elders. As I think back on those pieces of wisdom, I see a unique similarity among the different families' counsel. I don't believe it was an ethnic similarity, as Puerto

Rican families. I believe it was sage advice from parents who cared for their kids.

As the four of us reached our teenage years, our times together took on a greater value and sense of urgency. So many things were coming at us. It wasn't only girls, high school, and sex we worried about back then, just as you do now, it was thinking about our plans, beyond high school, that started to influence our everyday actions.

What were we going to be when we grew up? At what point were we supposed to start getting serious about some girl and make joint plans for the future? How important was it for us to worry about any of that? Were we too young to add that pressure to ourselves? Who knew? We had very little outside guidance on any of those questions.

I'm thankful that throughout the years of fun and amongst the occasional periods of confusion that we suffered through as kids, a few things remained constant. We tried our best to take care of each other and learn from each other.

Jimmy was our teacher when it came to morals and non-violence. If you felt like committing some childish prank, especially if it meant that someone's private property would be damaged; it didn't happen when Jimmy was around. When you hung out with Jimmy, you didn't even steal candy from the candy store. That's the way it was and always had to be around Jimmy.

Jimmy was the kid who couldn't keep a straight face when you tried to sneak a lie past your parents or teachers. He couldn't keep a straight face; he'd laugh and you were busted. Jimmy didn't copy anyone's homework either and he never gave you the answers to a test.

My friend Jimmy was also a soft-spoken kid. He didn't like arguments and he rarely raised his voice. I remember arguing with one of my girlfriends out in public; it was one of only a few times Jimmy ever got in my face. We were hanging out at a neighborhood park when I started to say some nasty things to the girl. Jimmy walked between us, looked me straight in the face, and said, "Bro, that's foul. Cut it out!" The look on his face told me he was disappointed in me and that he was serious about my shutting up.

I shut up and walked away. Not because Jimmy was right, he was. Not because I was scared that Jimmy and I would get into a fight, we wouldn't. I shut up and walked away because I didn't want to disappoint my friend, Jimmy.

I saw Jimmy intervene like that on many occasions. Even in potentially violent situations, Jimmy would get between the parties and prevent any further problems. I never saw Jimmy hit anyone.

Jimmy Jimenez was a good kid that grew up to be a good man and one of my heroes.

Felix Salgado, Mike, and I were a few degrees off from Jimmy's compass. As kids, we got in trouble more often than not. I wish I could blame Felix for all the trouble we got into but I can't. Mike and I had a habit of getting into hassles with kids from other neighborhoods and then having to go get reinforcements. Felix was like the cavalry. He'd ride in and save the day – usually bringing some extra support, tough dudes from his neighborhood.

Felix was a tough kid. I remember our 4th grade class' reenactment of the American Civil War. Felix insisted on being a "Rebel" from the South. He wanted to prove that he could have won the war if the right tactics were used. It was hard to argue his point of view, as our makeshift battlefield was 111th Street between Park and Lexington Avenues. He was a tough General Robert E. Lee and even harder to capture.

Felix taught us how to put up a good fight, defend a sound issue during a debate, and to retreat when the odds were too far on the other side. He would often say, "Believe in what you fight for, stand your ground, but be smart about it!" That quiet, yet strong resolve has been consistent throughout his life.

Felix joined the U.S. Marine Corps shortly after his graduation from high school. In 1966, the United States was in the middle of a conflict in Southeast Asia. (The term conflict was used in place of war; a declaration of war must be approved by Congress) Felix believed he had to serve his country in that struggle. He returned home years later; scarred physically and emotionally but proud of his service.

Over the years since his return, the pain from his wounds has never forced him to retreat from his basic rule – Believe in what you fight for, stand your ground but be smart about it! Felix wears a purple pin on his left lapel; it symbolizes the Purple Heart he was awarded during the Vietnam conflict. The pin is a quiet symbol. Felix is one of my heroes.

Brother John Tracy, a member of the Order of Irish Christian Brothers, was our 8th grade teacher at Commander Shea Parochial School – a really tough job. Commander Shea was in the middle of El Barrio. Imagine trying to educate inner-city kids who lived hard lives, had hard attitudes and very little vision beyond the ghetto. Some of my classmates would be best described as little thugs. The job wasn't impossible; it just required a lot of patience and commitment.

Brother Tracy dealt with all of the inner-city crap that invaded our childhood. Yet, he held up a light of hope for us. His manner was not obvious; but he let us know in so many ways that we could grow to be something beyond our imagination. He was tough on anyone that accepted "status quo," same stuff, different day.

As eighth-graders from a parochial school in New York City, you didn't attend a middle school the following year; you went straight to high school. Students within New York City had several options for high school. Besides the regular academic neighborhood schools within the city's five boroughs, there were vocational schools concentrating on aviation, maritime, automotive, fashion design, and industrial arts. Highly technical schools, such as the Bronx School of Science, were also available.

Brother Tracy made an extraordinary effort over the course of our last year in elementary school to make sure we chose our high school carefully. He helped Felix with his application to Rice H.S.

and Mike with his application to Cardinal Hayes H.S., both excellent schools.

Brother Tracy knew Jimmy and I were interested in aviation and aerospace and he helped us make the right choice. Aviation High School in Queens, New York had some of the toughest, pre-enrollment aptitude testing requirements of any school in the City. He met with our parents and explained the school's curriculum. He painted a clear picture of how our future would be tailored according to our studies in aviation.

Brother Tracy spoke at length, with Jimmy and me, making sure we understood the level of college preparatory work done at Aviation High. Tough academics – no slacking off! Then he worked with us as we went through the application and admission processes. Fortunately, Jimmy and I were both accepted. Everything that Brother Tracy had prepared us for happened. Everything we experienced prepared us for the careers in aviation and aerospace that Jimmy and I choose.

I had no better teacher throughout all my years of schooling including my undergraduate and graduate degrees than Brother John Tracy. He's one of my heroes.

Not all of the people I consider my heroes, were heroes during my youth. Some became so during my adulthood. My childhood friends Lila, Bonnie, and Alicia became heroes to me long after my teen years.

These three women often thought of as stereotypical products of broken homes, poverty, ghetto environments, and public subsistence, somehow saw hope beyond the horizons of inner-city life. Three women, who married very young, gave birth to their children while very young, and were divorced when they were just as young, shared all the ingredients for repeating the cycle of poverty they knew as children.

Nevertheless, they rose above the stereotypical expectations of society and used their inner-strengths to make a home for their kids, homes that opened the doors of opportunity for themselves and their families.

Lila, Bonnie, and Alicia are hard working and independent women, whom instilled standards of excellence in their children. They used themselves as an example of someone who takes responsibility for one's own actions and fate and then moves forward. Today, the children of these three women are well educated, professional, and career-oriented – the cycle of poverty is broken!

Lila, Bonnie, and Alicia are my heroes too.

I've left my Number One hero for last. Do you remember that little, red-haired girlfriend of mine from my teen years? Her name was Felicita Maldonado. Her name has been Felicita Alicea since 1966 as my partner, my best friend, my wife, and mother of our children.

Some of you might think I call my wife my number one hero just to be a nice guy. Think again!

Felicita stuck by my side when I was a confused teenager. She asked me to change the course I was on when I was wasting my life away inside many bottles of booze, and she stuck by me as I dragged myself away from those bottles.

She didn't drink and she didn't do drugs; yet, she never looked down her nose at anyone who did. She was what she was; a plain, freckled-face, curly-haired girl who expected all the other kids to do what was best for themselves and each other.

So how did we come to be married? That's a long story but I'll try to cut it down to the important points. She believed in me, my dreams and in her own dreams too.

Felicita knew that my life had taken a big turn following the car accident. She had heard of my dreams of being in the Air Force, of becoming an officer, and of a career in the military. She knew I had a vision of a better future than what my life would be like in the Bronx. She too had a vision of a better future.

In short order, Felicita and I grew closer. Eventually, we married, had good jobs on Wall Street, and started raising a family. However, the life we led was not the life we really wanted for each other or for our children. Don't get me wrong, we had a nice apartment in the Bronx. We made enough money to pay our bills and still enjoy New York for its Broadway theaters, museums and restaurants; but that wasn't enough.

We soon began to examine our options. Felicita forced me to look back to the dreams I had of a military career. She was the first to acknowledge the potential separations we would suffer. She even acknowledged that since the Vietnam conflict was still unsettled, I might be sent to Southeast Asia. Felicita calmly said, "Go do it! It's what you really want and it's what will be best for our family. I'll be fine. Go do it!"

I did do it! I joined the Air Force as an enlisted man, finished college, and attended Officer Training School. I was commissioned as a Second Lieutenant in 1977 and served a total of twenty-one years in the military.

Throughout all those years, Felicita stuck by me. We moved fourteen times during my Air Force career. Our children attended a long list of schools throughout the United States and Europe. All the while, Felicita raised our children, developed her own career, and considered all our moving as an adventure. Did we suffer separations? Yes, too many! The hardest was a one-year separation while I was stationed in Alaska and my family had to stay in Colorado.

Thirty-two years after we were married, Felicita and I found ourselves in a conversation about life in New York City. I told her that even as a kid, I never expected to live my whole life in New York. She was surprised to hear me say that; just as surprised as I was to hear her say that as a kid she too had never thought of New York as a permanent place.

Somehow, we had managed to find each other as kids, create a bond between us as teenagers, fall in love, get married, grow up together, stand by each other, and point each other in a mutual direction. Two kids with a vision of something beyond the horizons.

No doubt, Felicita is my Number One hero!

I know that finding true friends and heroes is a life-long challenge. Consider the following analogy as a tool you might use to answer that challenge.

I'm sitting at my desk, writing what I believe are the final pages of this book. I stopped writing a few moments ago and I found myself staring at three pencils I placed at the edge of the desk.

The first pencil is brand new; I just took it out of its original package. The eraser is clean and untouched. The tip of the pencil is blunt, waiting for me to use my pencil sharpener.

The second pencil is old. The point is dull and rounded. The eraser is worn all the way down to the metal band that holds the eraser onto the pencil's wood shaft. The pencil also has teeth marks along what's left of the short shaft; I must have bitten the pencil when I was stuck in deep thought.

The third pencil has also been used. However, the point has been sharpened. The eraser is still in good shape as is the shaft of the pencil, no teeth marks. This pencil is ready for my use.

An analogy has come to me as I look at these pencils as one group. Ask yourself which one of those three pencils represents your spirit. Once you've done that, ask yourself the same question about the spirits of your friends and those people you consider heroes.

Is your spirit like the new pencil, never sharpened, never used, and never tested? Is your spirit just sitting there waiting? Waiting for what? Are you expecting some sort of special invitation addressed to you, inviting you to join in on life, as life should be – Good? Here's a bit of advice, don't sit on anything hot while you're waiting for an invitation. That invitation doesn't come in the mail from someone else; you make that invitation. You make life happen!

Is your spirit more like the second pencil, worn and chewed up? Somewhere, in your young years, your spirit joined in on life; but somehow, your spirit lost its sharp point. You tried life and it didn't give you the answers you wanted. So, you chewed on the pencil as you contemplated life's mysteries and pondered on what move you would make next. Is that all your spirit is going to contribute to this life, chewing and pondering?

Please tell me that your spirit is more like the third pencil. Tell me that your spirit is strong, vibrant, and active and that its point is sharp – a viable spirit. Sure, your point, as the second pencil's point has been used, it has experience. However, unlike pencil number one, whose spirit is untried and pencil number two whose spirit sits and ponders; your spirit remains sharp, ready to open itself up to life.

I've shared with you many private moments during this book. I've opened my life to you about the lives of many of the people who influenced my growing up. I hope you realize that each of those people, whose life I touched or whose life touched me, shared their spirit with me.

I won't tell you that I've always stayed away from people whose spirits were like pencils number one or two. However, I will tell you that I've learned to surround myself, both personally and professionally, with people whose spirits are most like pencil number three.

I believe that it's people whose spirits are brave, strong, and ready to experience life – spirits that are good – that should fill your life.

I've told you about some of my heroes. I'm sure you'll discover your own. I hope that they'll each have a vision you understand and share, and a style that builds your character and theirs, not one that makes a lot of noise in the crowd. The heroes you choose don't need to be just like you. Actually, that's probably the last thing you want. Their uniqueness, those rare qualities they possess that attract you and urge you to learn from them, should be what sets them apart from other people. Make them your heroes.

"We call that person who has lost his father, an orphan; and a widower, that man who has lost his wife. But that man who has known the immense unhappiness of losing a friend, by what name do we call him? Here every language is silent and holds its peace in impotence."

Joseph Roux

Chapter Thirteen
One Last Story...A Special Dedication to Jimmy

A very tragic event in my life occurred during the final days of completing the initial draft of this book. My wife called me at my office to relay a message she had just received from our friends in New Jersey. She asked me to close the door to my office and sit down. Obviously, the news was serious and I did as she asked. Felicita then told me that one of my best friends, Jimmy Jimenez, had suffered a heart attack and died.

I'm sitting in an airplane, on my way back home from New Jersey, as I write these words. I want to share this moment in my life with you because I truly feel it sums up what I have spoken about in this book. I also need to tell you for my own sake. This is my personal goodbye to Jimmy.

Jimmy died quickly and unexpectedly on February 4, 2001. He was fifty-two years old. When I arrived at his home in New Jersey and embraced Judy, his widow, she asked me if I would consider speaking at Jimmy's funeral services. She said that he would've liked that. She had told everyone that if there was anyone that would speak at the services about Jimmy, it was to be me.

As accustomed as I am to public speaking, speaking at the funeral of someone you love is not the same – Not even close. Through many tears, I said the following words to a chapel full of people who had come to pay their respects to my friend.

"Ladies and Gentlemen, our Nation's flag is draped over Jimmy's casket in honor of his service to our Country. The flag's field of stars is displayed differently than you normally see it. Today, the stars are over Jimmy's heart, as a sign of honor and respect.

There are two military detachments present today representing the U.S. Marine Corps and the U.S. Air Force; the two services Jimmy was a member of during his military career. These fine, young Americans come to honor Jimmy as well, and they will conduct the military ceremony you will witness today. It is a ceremony with a proud tradition to honor a fallen comrade.

I've known Jimmy since the 1st grade. We went through grammar school and high school together so I can say I knew him well. We were like brothers.

I knew him to be someone who understood, very early in his life, that he had to pick his own path; he had to do right. He understood that everything he did in life would define his character, his future, and his legacy.

Jimmy defined his character by being a good kid that grew up to be a good man. He was a man of dignity. If he made a promise, you could carve it in stone because he would complete that promise.

Jimmy didn't believe in violence. I can't recall Jimmy ever raising his hand in anger to anyone. He preferred to step in and stop an argument than to stand by and let it escalate.

He was a man of service and commitment. He used his skills to serve his Country while he wore a uniform and then continued to use them in private industry. He took good care of his family and his friends.

Jimmy's insistence on doing things right was the foundation he set for his life's work. He did his best in school. He did his best while in the military. Moreover, he did his best in his civilian career. His best brought success to him and security to his wife and children. He did his best because that's the kind of man he was.

Jimmy's family is not the only legacy he leaves us. His example taught me what being an honorable man meant. I will always carry that with me as his legacy. Your memories of him as well as your presence here today are also part of Jimmy's legacy. I ask that you think about the steps you take in your life and how they will define your character, your future and your legacy. If you do that, you will truly honor Jimmy."

The sound of Taps soon filled the chapel. Those unforgettable notes were followed by the sounds of sharp verbal commands being given to the Honor Guard's rifle team. Each command was answered with a volley from the rifles – a twenty-one gun salute.

Two Marines removed the flag from Jimmy's casket. They folded the flag in the traditional pyramid shape and very solemnly transferred the flag into the arms of Air Force Master Sergeant Donald Newlin. MSgt Newlin then presented the flag to Judy Jimenez and her two sons, Mathew and Mark. He bent close to them and spoke in a whisper, the words that only they needed to hear. Words that will forever brighten the memory of that dark and sad day with thoughts of honor, honors given to a fallen comrade, a friend, a father, and a husband.

Dear Reader, it will be a long time before tears stop coming to my eyes every time I think of Jimmy. I lost a friend, a brother. I'm profoundly grateful for what he taught me. I wish each of you that same legacy.

"He who has done his best for his own time has lived for all times."

Johann von Schiller

About the Author

    Joseph Alicea was born in New York City and was raised in areas known as Spanish Harlem and the South Bronx. Those were neighborhoods whose streets, parks, schools, and apartment buildings existed in perpetual decline. Sadly, most visitors suspected the inhabitants themselves were in equal decline. Whatever promise, if any, the future held for kids growing up in those ghettos was questionable; survival was their first priority. Joe and many of his friends took the best out of every experience from school, family, friendships, and the streets. They took control of their lives. They are survivors.

Joe left New York City and joined the U.S. Air Force. Along the way, he earned a BS in Aeronautical Sciences and an MS in Business Management. He went from Enlisted man to Officer and traveled with his family around the world to places they had only dreamed of while living in the Bronx. Over the last twenty years, Joe has demonstrated a selfless commitment to mentoring programs for young adults. He has spent countless hours with middle and high school children in Europe and the United States counseling, teaching, coaching, and helping them understand that they too can reach for the stars.